COLLINS GEM

WHISKY

Carol P. Shaw

HarperCollins*Publishers*

HarperCollins Publishers
P O Box, Glasgow G4 0NB

First published 1993

Reprint 10 9 8 7 6

ISBN 0 00 470121 6

The publishers would like to acknowledge the
assistance of distillers, independent bottlers and
trade associations while compiling this book.

Printed in Italy by Amadeus S.p.A.

Contents

The history of whisky making in Scotland

It is widely accepted that whisky has been distilled in Scotland for hundreds of years, and different hypotheses as to its origins have been suggested. Some state that it was brought into the country by missionary monks from Ireland; others point out that, as the Arabs were among the first to learn distillation techniques, knights and men returning from the Crusades could have brought the knowledge back with them. It may well be, however, that it evolved simply as a means of using up

Lagavulin Distillery, Islay

5

barley which would otherwise have been ruined after a wet harvest.

The name itself is derived from the Gaelic, *uisge beatha*, meaning 'water of life'. The Latin equivalent, *aqua vitae*, was a term which was commonly used throughout Europe to describe the local spirit. *Aqua vitae* made its first appearance in official Scottish records in 1494, with the record of malt being sold to one Friar John Cor with which to make the spirit, but *uisge* seems to have first been mentioned in the account of the funeral and wake of a Highland chieftain around 1618. The amount of whisky making throughout Scotland increased greatly during the seventeenth century, and nowhere more so than in the Highlands. In fact, so enthusiastic was the growth in distillation that before the end of the sixteenth century there had already been complaints in Parliament that so much barley was being used in whisky production that it was in short supply as a foodstuff! These distillers' method was basic and simple: a sack of barley might be soaked in water — for example, in a burn — for a day or two, then the barley would be spread out in a dry place, allowing it to sprout, for around ten days. The sprouting would be halted by drying the barley over a peat fire (peat being used as the main source of fuel in the Highlands). It was then put in a container with boiling water and yeast, to ferment. This mix would be passed twice through a

pot still, emerging as whisky at the other end. These distillers had to be fairly skilled at their job, to possess the judgement to know when to take off the middle cut of the spirit (the drinkable part), avoiding the poisonous foreshots, at the start of the distillation, and the lower-quality feints, or aftershots, at the end. Although they had no instruments, methods did evolve of testing the whisky's strength, including setting fire to the spirit to measure the amount of liquid left behind, and mixing it with gunpowder to see how it reacted when ignited — if the gunpowder-and-whisky cocktail exploded, it was known that the whisky was too strong!

It was during the seventeenth century, too, that the first tax on whisky was introduced by Parliament, because of the pressing need to raise revenue to finance the army fighting in the English Civil War in 1644.

Although it was reduced under the Commonwealth after the king's execution, this episode effectively marked the beginning of the principle of the taxation of whisky.

The union of Scotland and England in 1707, however, heralded some changes for the whisky industry, and few of them were constructive. A malt tax was introduced in 1725 which adversely affected the quality of beer — until then the most popular drink — and of whiskies produced by the professional commercial distillers in the more populous Lowlands, who were obliged to produce whiskies of poorer quality, with less malted barley content. These taxes also applied to Highland malt whisky, but in that still-inaccessible region it was much easier to ignore, and illicit distillation continued to flourish. This attempt at revenue raising, affecting the Lowland distillers but ignored in the Highlands, set a pattern for the rest of the century.

The large distillers in the Lowlands continued successfully to produce rough grain whisky whose quantity was more important than its quality, for consumption locally and in England, where it was often used as a basis for cheap gin. However, pressure from the English distillers, who were being undercut by Scottish imports flooding the market, encouraged Parliament to introduce a series of increasingly draconian taxes against the Scots whisky. The small distillers in the Highlands —

most of whom were probably farmers and crofters, pursuing a lucrative sideline — continued to make superior quality whisky without paying tax. Much of this whisky was brought to the Lowlands for sale, where it was more popular with those who could afford it than the rougher spirit produced by the Lowland distillers. The government in London had no answer to the problems they had helped create in the whisky industry, other than to raise taxes still further, making the law seem more and more ineffectual.

Finally, however, pressure on the government brought an abandonment of its futile attempts at taxation and regulation. A Royal Commission was set up to investigate the industry, the Excise service in the Highlands was strengthened, and in 1822 an act was passed which brought harsher penalties for those found to be operating unlicensed stills. The following year the Excise Act made an attempt to encourage licensed distilling, cutting both duty and restrictions on exports to England. Now, an annual licence of £10 was introduced on stills over 40 gallons (smaller stills were not allowed), and a more modest duty of 2/3d per gallon of whisky brought in. The Duke of Gordon, whose estates included the Glenlivet area, was a prime mover in the reforms, and he encouraged his tenants, including George Smith, producer of the whisky which came to be known as The Glenlivet, to take out licences.

Laphroaig Distillery, Islay

The new act was effective and successful, and the amount of legally distilled whisky consumed had risen threefold by 1827.

Freed from its legislative shackles, the whisky industry was able to concentrate on the development of its product and markets. The product itself was given an impetus by the invention by Aeneas Coffey, an Irish former exciseman, of a new still which he patented in 1832; this allowed the distillation of grain whisky to take place in a continuous process in one still. The new process cut back on costs, allowing the Lowland grain distillers to use even less malted barley than before, and to produce on an even bigger scale. Ironically, however, the success of the Excise Act and the new patent still brought trouble for the industry in the mid nineteenth century, because of overproduction and despite the exploiting of new export markets in the Empire and overseas. This development saw the fore-shadowing of the emergence of the Distillers Company, with the combining in a price-fixing cartel of the six biggest Lowland grain whisky producers; they were not to join together officially, however, until 1877, by which time the face of the industry had changed dra-matically.

This change was brought about by the development of techniques of blending malt and grain whiskies to produce a lighter spirit than the traditional single malt, and a more flavoursome one than grain whisky. In the 1850s Andrew Usher, the Edinburgh whisky mer-chant who was agent for the Glenlivet whiskies, had vatted together several casks of Glenlivet from his stocks, producing in the process a more consistent product. The practice was soon extended to the blend-ing of malt and grain. This was held to produce a lighter spirit which English drinkers, unused to the much stronger malt product of the pot still, found much more palatable. It also introduced an element of consistency to the product. Coincidentally, this development came when reserves of brandy, the first-choice spirit in England, were threatened as a result of the Phylloxera blight in the French vineyards in the 1860s. Timely exploitation of the market in England by the grain producers and blenders meant that, as stocks of brandy declined in the 1870s and '80s, the new blended whiskies came to take their place as the quality spirit, and the 1890s was a period of unprecedented growth for the Scottish whisky industry. New malt distilleries were opened and groups like Distillers and the North British Distillery Company, serving the interests of the grain distillers and the blenders respectively, became phenomenally successful. The whisky industry was developing to become recognizable as the industry it is today.

The boom period was followed, typically, by a slump, and difficult times for the industry at the beginning of this century were compounded by the First World War and the introduction of Prohibition in the USA in 1920. The years from then to the Second World War saw a drop in output of almost 50%, and an almost complete halt being brought to the production of malt whisky. This situation continued after the war when, naturally, what grain was available had to be diverted to feed the people rather than make whisky. As prosperity returned in the 1950s, whisky output increased and exports rose. New distilleries were built in the '60s, old ones reopened, and the production of malt whisky quadrupled in a decade. Take-over and consolidation were the keynotes of the industry in the 1970s, with English brewers moving into the whisky market on a large scale. This trend culminated in the messy take over of the Distillers Company (now United Distillers) by Guinness, a transaction which resulted in the chairman of the brewing giant and several of his advisers ending up in jail. Ironically, however, the adage of there being no bad publicity seems to be borne out by the Distillers take over: an episode which apparently brought the industry into disrepute, came at a time when the market was picking up again after the slump of the mid '70s–mid '80s, and served to give whisky a timely publicity boost.

This upturn in the drink's fortunes has continued to the present day, with the emphasis in marketing now on quality rather than quantity: cheaper blends have tended to disappear, single malts are taking an increasing share of the market, and price rises are being met by consumers, who seem to prefer the new expensive-and-exclusive image of the drink. Marketing has responded accordingly, with increasing importance being placed on packaging and advertising, and with the opening of new visitor centres in the distilleries themselves. Export markets, too, are flourishing, particularly in Japan, and the present buoyancy in the industry looks set to continue — something which can only be good for all those who appreciate and love good whisky.

Above: Lagavulin Distillery, Islay
Opposite: Cardhu Distillery, Moray

Cutting the peat

Two different processes are used for the distillation of malt and grain whiskies.

How whisky is made

MALT WHISKY In malt whisky distillation, there are several basic steps to the process: malting, mashing, fermentation, distillation and maturation, although the minor elements may vary from one distillery to another. Barley may be bought in pre-malted, but if it is not, it is first filtered to remove any foreign matter.

1) *Malting* The process begins when the barley is transferred to soak in tanks of water which go by the self-explanatory name of barley steeps; this process takes two to four days. In the traditional process, the barley is then spread on a malting floor, to be turned by hand daily for the next twelve days or so, allowing it to sprout; now, however, most distilleries use mechanical devices for turning the sprouting barley. As the seeds germinate, the starch in the barley releases some of its sugars. At the appropriate moment, germination is stopped by drying the cereal in a malt kiln over a peat furnace or fire. The peat smoke which flavours the drying barley at this stage can, depending on its intensity, be tasted in the final whisky itself. The malt kilns traditionally had the pagoda-style roofs which were such an instantly recognizable characteristic of the malt distilleries; these can still be seen on older distilleries.

17

2) Mashing The next stage for the malted barley is passage through a mill, from which it emerges roughly ground as grist. From here it is moved to a mash tun, a large vat where it is mixed with hot water and agitated, so that its sugars dissolve to produce wort, a sweet, non-alcoholic liquid.

Washbacks where the liquid is fermented to produce wash
Images courtesy of The Scotch Whisky Association

How malt whisky is made

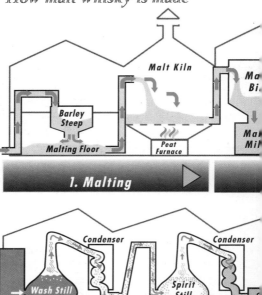

Malt Kiln

Barley Steep

Malting Floor

Peat Furnace

Ma...
Bi...

Ma...
Mil...

1. Malting ▶

Condenser

Condenser

Wash Still

Spirit Still

Furnace

Furnace

4. Distillation

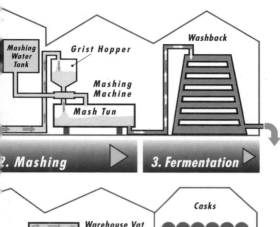

Mashing Water Tank

Grist Hopper

Washback

Mashing Machine

Mash Tun

2. Mashing ▷

3. Fermentation ▷

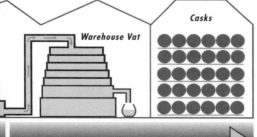

Warehouse Vat

Casks

5. Maturation ▷

This process is repeated to ensure that all the sugars have been collected. The solid remains of the barley are removed at this point for conversion to cattle food.

3) Fermentation The wort is cooled and transferred to washbacks, large vats where yeast is added and the process of fermentation begins. The chemical reaction which takes place with the addition of the yeast converts the sugars in the wort to alcohol, a process which takes around two days and results in a low-strength alcoholic liquid now called wash.

4) Distillation The wash is then ready for the stills. The shape of the still is one of the most important factors in the whisky-making process, as it can have a decisive influence on the final character of the malt whisky: for instance, a still with a short neck will produce a whisky with heavier oils and a more intense flavour, whereas lighter-flavoured whiskies with less heavy oils will emerge from a still with a long or high neck.

The first still which the wash passes through is known, appropriately, as the wash still, and here it is heated. As the alcohol has a lower boiling point than water, the alcoholic steam rises up the still through its long spout to the worm, a condensing coil. The distillate, now called low wines, is passed into the second still, the spirit still, where the process is repeated, with the liquid running off into the glass-fronted spirit safe.

It is at this point that the skill of the distiller is crucial: unable to smell or taste the liquid to judge it, he must know when to separate the middle cut, or main run of the spirit, which contains the best-quality alcohol needed for malt whisky, from the foreshots (the raw, poisonous first distillate) and the feints, or aftershots, which contain a lower grade of alcohol. Once separated, foreshots and feints are fed back into the wash for redistillation.

5) *Maturation* The main run of the alcohol is now transferred for storage to a vat and mixed with water to bring it down in strength. It is then transferred into casks for maturing. The whole process of distillation can theoretically be completed inside a week, but the whisky must now mature for at least three years before it can be sold; during this time, a small percentage of the whisky, known as the 'angels' share', will evaporate. In practice, malt whiskies are left to mature for an average of eight to fifteen years.

GRAIN WHISKY With the exception of the Invergordon Distillery, all grain distilleries are located in the Lowlands. Grain distilleries use patent (or Coffey) stills, which can operate continuously. The basic process used is similar to that for malt, up to the point of distillation, although everything takes place on a much larger scale, and with much less malted barley: maize, unmalted barley or other cereals are generally used.

Distillation is carried out in two large cylindrical columns which are linked by pipes. The wash passes into the first column, the rectifier, in a coiled pipe running through its length. Jets of steam are forced up into the column, through a series of perforated plates between which the coiled pipe passes, heating the wash inside before it passes out and into the analyser. In the analyser the wash is no longer in the coiled pipe, and it is now met by another jet of steam passing through more perforated plates. The steam and evaporated alcohol rise and are passed back into the rectifier, with the alcohol cooling as it moves up, encountering fresh, cold wash in the coiled pipe on its way down, until it reaches a cold water coil where it condenses before passing out of the still. The impure alcohols in the first and last part of the distillate can be redistilled, while the alcohol which reaches the spirit safe and receiver is very pure. The whisky will mature faster than malt, and is less subject to variable factors. The vast majority of the produce will go for blending not long after its three-year maturation period has passed.

Opposite & overleaf: The blenders at work
Images courtesy of The Scotch Whisky Association

Blending

Blending is a slightly separate part of the whisky-making process, with a third product being made from malt and grain whiskies. It both guarantees consistency of the brand and aims to create a new whisky of character in its own right. It is a process

which absorbs by far the greater part of the distilleries' production, and is the mainstay of the industry.

The process was developed on a commercial footing in the second half of the nineteenth century. Although it may initially have been used as a way of stretching further supplies of the more expensive malt whisky, it was the means by which whisky was popularized first in the English market, then overseas.

Blending is an olfactory craft, with blenders nosing rather than tasting whiskies. It is a highly skilled profession, with anything from 20–50 different whiskies being mixed in any one brand, including varieties of

type, region, distillery and age. The new whisky's character is dependent on how well these different component whiskies complement and contrast with one another to bring out their various flavours. The high number of component whiskies is the blender's guarantee of consistency: if one contributing distillery goes out of production, the consistency of the blend can be maintained more easily than if there were a lesser number of whiskies, each with a stronger presence, as ingredients.

The ingredients and their proportions are closely guarded secrets, although it is generally assumed that where a blender owns a distillery, the distillery's produce will be represented to some degree in the blend: so, for example, the produce of Laphroaig Distillery, which is owned by Allied Distillers, is present in their Long John, Black Bottle, Ballantine's and Teacher's blends. The produce of some distilleries is never bottled as a single malt, and goes entirely for blending.

After the whiskies are matured, they are mixed together in their correct proportions in a vat, then 'married' in oak casks for at least a year to allow intermingling and further maturation to take place. As with most malts, the blend is reduced to the correct strength by the addition of water. Burnt-sugar caramel may be added to bring a blend up to its desired colour before the whisky is filtered, bottled and labelled.

There are particular legal constraints on what can be termed Scotch whisky, the most basic of which dictate the components of the whisky (cereals, malt and yeast), the maximum alcoholic strength at distillation (94.8% alcohol by volume), and the minimum length of maturation (at least three years). Finally, the whisky itself must have been distilled and matured in Scotland.

Different types of whisky

Scotland produces two main types of whisky, and all the available varieties of the spirit are variations on these themes. The first is malt whisky, made from malted barley, using a pot still; and the second is grain whisky, made from other cereals — maize or unmalted barley, together with a little malted barley — in a patent still. The two types' distillation processes are explained on pp. 17–24; what follows here is an explanation of the varieties in which they are available.

Single malt is the product of one distillery. Legally, it can be sold after only three years' maturation, but in practice it is generally left to mature from between eight to fifteen years, by which time its character and flavour has become more pronounced and rounded. Generally, whiskies of varying proof strengths and ages from different casks are mixed together, ensuring a consistent distillery product (as the product of any one distillation will inevitably not be identical to any other), although the age which appears on the label is always the age of the youngest distillation in the bottle. Malts are diluted from their cask strength (up to mid 60s percentage alcohol by volume) to 40% or 43% for commercial marketing. Single malts comprise a relatively small, although increasing, proportion of the total whisky market.

A sub-group of single malt whisky is the **single-cask malt**. Generally available commercially only through specialist shops and independent merchants (see pp. 50–52), these are whiskies which, as the name suggests, are the produce of one distillation, bottled straight from the cask and not vatted with any other produce from the distillery. This process, together with the absence of chill filtration before the whiskies are bottled, ensures that the particular character of a distillery's whisky — and, indeed, of a specific distillation — is unmasked, and greatly emphasized. Supplies of a particular variety or distillation are, by nature, finite. This is the most expensive type of whisky, often costing at least double the price of a normal, distillery-bottled single malt, but felt by many whisky drinkers to be well worth the expense.

A **vatted malt** is the final of the malt whisky subgroups. This type of whisky has a long pedigree, having formed the basis of the first blended whisky in the mid nineteenth century. Vatted malts are normally produced by blenders and big companies who have a variety of malt distilleries from which to take their product. It could be regarded as a half-way house between a blend and a single malt, although the flavours in some vatted malts can be just as well developed as those in a single. Single malts of different distilleries and different ages are mixed together, the age (if any) on the label being that of the youngest whisky in the mixture. The words 'vatted malt' normally do not appear on a label; instead, the absence of the word 'single' before 'malt', together with an absence of a distillery name, is generally an indicator of a vatted malt.

Grain whisky has been mentioned briefly above, and in proportion to the quantities in which it is produced, very little of it is bottled in its own right. Instead, its main function is as a component part of the **blend**. Blended whiskies are a mixture of malt and grain, not necessarily in any fixed proportions but rather in a recipe which will achieve the blender's desired balance in terms of character, cost and quality. Blends were the means in the nineteenth century by which hitherto too-strongly flavoured malt whiskies were mellowed for the palate in markets outside Scotland — firstly for England, then for export markets. The desired aim of a blender is not to dilute or diminish the flavours of the various component whiskies, but rather to choose ones which are both compatible and complementary, resulting in the creation of a new whisky of distinctive character. In this way, consistency of the product can also be assured. Blended whiskies, of which there are over a thousand, comprise the greater part of the whisky market. The major blenders generally own both malt and grain distilleries, so it is safe to assume that the product of a particular malt distillery will be represented to some degree in its owner's blends.

A **de luxe** whisky is a particular type of blend, recognized to be of superior quality to a standard blend. De luxe whiskies generally contain a higher proportion of malt which is older, more mature and consequently more expensive. Some de luxes carry an age statement on their label; as with other whiskies, this is the age of the youngest component in the bottle.

Blends, but of a quite different type, is a name which can be given to the growing market for whisky **liqueurs**. Some of these contain whisky flavoured with honey, fruits, herbs and spices, while the cream liqueurs also contain whisky, but are more inclined towards cream, coffee and chocolate in their flavours.

Regional characteristics of malt whisky

The qualities and characteristics associated with particular producing regions are not a result of current tastes and fashions, but rather a legacy of the past. In times when roads were often poor or, at some times of the year, non-existent, when communications were often difficult, sometimes dangerous and always time-consuming, and trade between different parts of the country was expensive, it was obvious that a distillery would use the raw materials and ingredients which were to hand in a particular locality rather than go to the trouble of importing produce from other areas. These factors, combined with local climate and geology, helped produce whiskies which varied in character from one part of the country to another.

The current chief distinction, between Highland and Lowland whiskies, is also a legacy of a past legal and fiscal policy. As a means of controlling the trade and movement of whisky from Highlands to Lowlands (whose cheaper, coarser grain spirit was then successfully being exported into England), the Highland dividing line was established, following roughly the Highland Boundary Fault Line, which runs from the Firth of Clyde to the Firth of Tay. The distinction remained, even with the equalizing of quality between malts from north and south of the line, and is still recognized today.

33

Existing distilleries featured in this book

ORKNEY

Kirkwall • Highland Park

John o' Groats

Wick •
Pulteney •

Pulteney

Old Pulteney

Balblair
Glenmorangie
Teaninich
Glen Ord
Nairn • Royal Brackla
Inverness •
Tomatin

Peterhead

Fraserburgh

Glenugie •
Glenglassaugh •
Macduff •

SPEYSIDE
(See pp. 40–41)

SKYE
Talisker

Lowland malts are defined as those coming from the southern half of Scotland – that is, from south of the Highland line. The area stretches from the southernmost distillery, Bladnoch in Wigtownshire, to Littlemill and Inverleven in Dunbartonshire, which are almost on the Highland line. In terms of their taste, the Lowland malts are perhaps a good first stepping stone into the wider world of malt whiskies for the drinker who wants to graduate from blends: relatively unassertive in character, they are generally soft and light, with a gentle sweetness which ensures them many fans among more experienced palates. Much of the produce of the Lowland malt distilleries is used in blends.

As a once-popular music-hall ditty more colourfully suggested, **Campbeltown** was a major centre of whisky production. Over 20 distilleries operated there in the later nineteenth century, encouraged by the abundance of local supplies of peat, barley from the Mull of Kintyre, and a nearby source of cheap coal. However, over-production, too-wide variations in quality and the exhaustion of the local coal seam contributed to the decline of the local industry, to the point where only two distilleries now remain. With the shift in emphasis from sea-borne to road traffic, it is unlikely that the town will ever again regain its former eminence. Nevertheless, it still retains its regional classification.

Campbeltown whiskies are generally accepted to be quite distinctive, with a character which is mellower than that of the Islay malts, with a smoothness and a variable peatiness in the flavour.

Islay malts must be, for everyone from the beginner to the connoisseur, the most distinctive of all single malt whiskies — certainly, their flavour is among the strongest of all the regions. Peat is the key, both in terms of its influence on the ingredients used for distillation and of its presence in the final taste. The island has extensive beds of peat, over which the water used in the distillation process flows, arriving at its destination already flavoured. Varying amounts of peat are also used to dry the barley. In the past this latter ingredient, too, was produced locally, although now it may be brought in. Peat is noticeable in the flavours of all the Islay malts, from the mildest to the most intensely flavoured, imparting a dryness which is sometimes balanced by sweetness, sometimes emphasized by smokiness. For beginners to single malts, the Islay whiskies seem like an acquired taste, but they are an essential ingredient in the whisky-blending process, and the chances are that what you may think of as the distinctively Scottish flavour in your whisky is imparted by their presence in a blend.

Finally, the largest region, with more distilleries than the rest of the country combined, is **Highland**, probably the quintessential Scottish whisky production area. This is the land which lies to the north of the Highland line and includes distilleries as far apart as Inchmurrin in Dunbartonshire, Oban in Argyll, Pulteney in Wick and Highland Park in Orkney. As might be expected across such a wide area, generalizations become less valid and sub-division becomes more necessary. Geographical divisions of north, south, east and west, together with a special one for Speyside, can be useful in illustrating particular characteristics.

The north Highland malts can be said to stretch from the area around Inverness up the east coast to Wick. The whiskies from this area are generally smooth, and while ranging from dry to fruity sweet, are not normally quite as peaty as some of their more southerly neighbours. Whisky from the southern Highlands — generally speaking, around the Perthshire area and to the west — is, as might be expected, softer and lighter in character, often reasonably sweet but with one or two dry examples. The western Highlands is the smallest of the Highland sub-divisions, encompassing the area from Oban to Fort William with their smooth, rounded whiskies. The eastern Highlands has distilleries spread out along the North Sea coast from Brechin in the south to Banff in the north. The whiskies in this area offer a wide range of styles, one of the widest of any of the sub-divisions, from fruity sweetness to peaty dryness.

A pair
of pot stills
Courtesy of The Scotch
Whisky Association

Existing Speyside distilleries featured in this book

Inchgower
Buckie
Glenglassaugh
Spey
Aultmore
Knockdhu
Strathisla
Auchroisk
Keith
Deveron
Glentauchers
Glen Keith
Glendronach
raigellachie
Convalmore
enie
Glenfiddich
wn
Glendullan
Huntly
et
Mortlach
Pittyvaich-Glenlivet
Fiddich
Ardmore

Image above and overleaf courtesy of The Scotch Whisky Association

The largest and most famous of the Highland subdivisions is that of Speyside, producing a range of single malts whose names are instantly recognizable, even to non-whisky drinkers: Macallan, Glenfiddich, Glenfarclas and Glenlivet. The area is concentrated around the Elgin–Dufftown district, a picturesque and fertile area whose remoteness made it an ideal location for the whisky smugglers of past centuries to escape the efforts of the excisemen. Speyside whiskies are recognized as being mellow, with a malty sweetness and light notes of peat: beyond this basic generalization, however, lies a wealth of variety and subtlety, and the Speyside malts can range from the aromatic and flowery to the robust and sherried. Whiskies can be found in this area to satisfy all palates, from the novice to the connoisseur, and for all occasions.

The final Highland sub-group is that of the Island whiskies. As might be expected when these are viewed on a map, the classification is not so much based on characteristics as convenience – this is a suitable sub-group in which to deal with the remaining whiskies which do not fit in any other. The islands concerned are Jura, Mull and Skye in the west, and Orkney in the north. (It does not, of course, include Islay, whose distinctive style merits a category of its own.) Once again, generalizations are difficult to make, with characters ranging from reasonably dry to full, sweet and malty.

On pp. 235–37 each malt whisky is listed in its area of production. As with any classification, these listings should not be taken as hard and fast rules — taste and preferences vary so greatly that they can only be general guidelines. The best way to decide how well particular whiskies fit their supposed regional listing or characteristic is simply to try each one for yourself!

With over 250,000 people visiting Scotland's distilleries every year, receiving visitors has become an important means of promotion and source of revenue for the more famous whisky makers. Most distilleries are happy to accept visitors, and you will find facilities ranging from a friendly, impromptu guided tour to a full-scale reception centre with video presentation, organized tour and gift shop.

Eight of the distilleries on Speyside have organized into a 70-mile-long Whisky Trail. These distilleries are generally attractive, and often have traditional features like pagodas or hand-turned malting floors. The pattern of a visit is similar in each: a welcome will be followed by a video and slide presentation, a guided tour with an explanation of the whisky-making process, and a free glass of the distiller's product, as well as the opportunity to purchase gifts in the distillery shop. The distilleries on the Trail are: Cardhu, Glenfarclas, Glenfiddich, Glen Grant, The Glenlivet, Strathisla, Tamdhu and Tamnavulin. Details of the Trail can be obtained from Scottish Tourist Board offices (head office, tel: 031-332 2433), the Scotch Whisky Heritage Centre (tel: 031-220 0441) or the Scotch Whisky Association (tel: 071-629 4384).

Whether you decide to visit a distillery on the

Whisky Trail or another which simply welcomes visitors, you can telephone in advance to find out the particular facilities at your chosen distillery — the telephone numbers of those distilleries which are equipped to receive visitors are given under their entries throughout the book. It is particularly advisable to telephone if you plan to visit during July and August. Although this is the height of the tourist season, it is also the traditional 'silent' period for this industry which was so closely associated with farming: closing the distillery at this time meant that the workers could help to gather in the harvest.

If you are in Edinburgh, a visit to the Scotch Whisky Heritage Centre on Castlehill is always a good starting point if you want to find out more about the industry, with exhibits which are both fun and educational. You can travel back through the industry's past, including the days of illicit distillation, viewing all from the comfort of your own motorized whisky cask!

Finally, for the opportunity to see a perfectly preserved traditional distillery, Dallas Dhu at Forres should not be missed if you are travelling through the north east. Established at the end of the nineteenth century, it stands in lovely countryside to the south of the town. It was previously owned by the Distillers Company, who closed it in 1983, and is now operated by the Historic Buildings and Monuments Commission for

Scotland. Although it no longer produces whisky, it offers one of the most interesting distillery visits in Scotland. (Visitors are welcome 1000–1900 1 Apr.–30 Sept. Tel: 0309-672802 for details.)

Distillery signs (above and right)
Blair Athol, Perthshire; Cardhu, Moray

Overleaf: Guard geese, Ballantine's Distillery, Dunbartonshire

As explained on pp. 29–30 single malts bottled by the distilleries are generally a marrying of casks from several distillations, with water being added to reduce the whisky to an agreed alcohol by volume strength for bottling. The whisky will also generally undergo a process of cold-temperature filtration to remove the residues which naturally precipitate cloudiness in the drink after dilution, when it is kept at low temperatures, or when it has ice added. Views differ as to whether this alters the character and taste of the whisky: the producers cite scientific evidence to show that there is no alteration to the whisky's character if it is not diluted below 40% alcohol by volume. However, various independent bodies believe that it does, and they offer consumers the chance to test for themselves.

The Scotch Malt Whisky Society (tel: 031-554 3452) is one of these bodies. It buys from the distilleries selected single malts which it bottles straight from the cask and offers to its members, of whom there are over 18,000 around the world. The society aims to promote the increased understanding, appreciation and discerning comsumption of malt whisky. The independent spirit merchants, William

Cadenhead Ltd (tel: 031-556 5864), also subscribe to this view of the chill-filtration process, and pride themselves on maintaining the individuality of each batch of whisky, bottling straight from the cask at cask strength. The company's approach, of minimal interference with the whisky, relatively simple packaging, and the taking of care over content rather than presentation, is designed to appeal to the slightly more experienced whisky drinker. Much of Cadenhead's stock comes from distilleries whose produce is not otherwise available to the public.

Gordon and MacPhail of Elgin (tel: 0343-545111) also offer a wide range of their own bottlings from many distilleries. The company, owned and run by the Urquhart family, was established in 1895 as a wine and spirit merchant and licensed grocers, and now is regarded as the world's leading malt whisky specialists. Gordon and MacPhail's policy has always been to buy new whisky direct from a distillery, often in their own casks, warehousing it themselves and bottling it when they consider it to be at its best. Each barrel is carefully assessed for quality, style and quantity available prior to bottling, thereby achieving a consistency and quality of malt for which the company is recognized. As well as single and vatted malts, cask-strength bottlings and unusual blends, they have a large selection of old and rare whiskies.

Finally, if you would like to know more about any aspect of Scotch whisky, the Scotch Whisky Association will happily supply information for you. The association aims to promote the interests of the Scotch whisky industry in Britain and around the world, and its membership comprises almost all companies involved in the industry. The Public Affairs office is in London (tel: 071-629 4384), while the head office is in Edinburgh (tel: 031-229 4383).

Distillery with pagoda-style roof
Image courtesy of The Scotch Whisky Association

The label on a whisky bottle will allow you to identify a few basic facts about its contents even before you open the bottle — most obviously, the brand and its producers, the type of whisky it is, and its age, quantity and strength. Single malts normally proclaim themselves as such, and the identification of the producing distillery acts as a double check. A label which states a bottle's contents to be malt, but without the words 'single' or 'unblended', is probably vatted. Grains and blends likewise will identify themselves, and while most de luxe whiskies will also do so, this is not always the case. Blends of all kinds will carry the name of the blenders rather than of any distillery.

Where whiskies carry an age statement on the label, this will be the age of the youngest whisky in the bottle. Instead of this, some malts may give the year of their distillation. Single malts are usually eight years old and upwards, becoming more expensive as their age increases. It is generally held, however, that up to fifteen years is a good maturation period for whisky, and while some whiskies improve by maturing beyond this period, not all do of necessity — it depends on the individual whisky. Whiskies for general consumption in the UK are normally packaged in 70 or 75 cl bottles, but you may also come upon 1 l bottles.

Most whiskies are sold at 40% alcohol by volume.

The system for measuring spirit strength in Britain changed in 1980 from the older and more complicated Sikes system of measuring proof strength, to the Organization of Legal Metrology, or OIML system, which measures spirit strength as a percentage of volume at 20 °C. Whisky is distilled at a much higher content than its final form for consumption. Water may be added before it goes into the cask, to bring it down to 68.5% alcohol by volume, a standard measure. Some evaporation takes place as the whisky matures, leaving a final cask strength of around 45–60%. Cask-strength whiskies are available, but most single malts have to have water added to bring them down to 40% or 43% (normally for the export market) strength for bottling. However, the industry may move towards a standard strength of 40% after a 1988 European Community directive which based the amount of duty on the alcoholic strength of a spirit. 40% alcohol by volume is equivalent to the old measure of 70 ° proof and, confusingly, 80 ° proof in the USA, which uses a slightly different system again.

PRODUCT OF SCOTLAND

BRUICHLADDICH
ISLAY

AGED **10** YEARS

SINGLE MALT
SCOTCH WHISKY

DISTILLED AND BOTTLED BY
BRUICHLADDICH DISTILLERY CO. LTD.
BRUICHLADDICH ISLE OF ISLAY

Founded 1881

70cl   Bottled in Scotland   40%vol

Left: Bruichladdich Single Malt, Islay

Below: Glenturret Single Malt, Highland

DISTILLED · MATURED · IN · OAK · CASKS · AND · BOTTLED · AT

The
GLENTURRET

ESTABLISHED · 1775

Single Highland Malt
SCOTCH WHISKY

AGED **12** YEARS

PRODUCT OF SCOTLAND
BOTTLED IN SCOTLAND

70cl ℮ 40%vol

THE · GLENTURRET · DISTILLERY · CRIEFF · SCOTLAND

Developing the palate

by

Una Holden-Cosgrove

Apart from the anatomical meaning – the roof of the mouth – a palate refers to the sense of taste, but the roof of the mouth does play an important role in discerning a taste. Spicy, hot and cold, pleasant and objectionable sensations are all in the province of the palate. Everyone has a different reaction to taste, and both physically and psychologically the sense of smell has a major influence on how these sensations are perceived.

Where whisky is concerned, a palate needs to be educated in the same way as it must gradually be introduced to the different foods encountered in different countries – after all, a vindaloo is hardly the best introduction to curries! Similarly, a dram of one whisky can never be regarded as a real experience or a satisfactory introduction to the elixir of life. Every whisky has a different taste and smell: some are quite fierce, or vigorous, and others more honeyed and enticing. To attempt one of the more powerful malts, such as The Glenlivet or Talisker, without any previous knowledge of whisky can only kill any interest in proceeding further.

Unfortunately the early writers on whisky overlooked the fact that their palates were accustomed to the differing tastes and had been conditioned so that the robust types were more to their particular liking. As a result the malts and blends they recommended so highly were usually too powerful for the beginner, leading to an undeservedly macho image for malt whisky which meant that these stronger whiskies were more commonly found on the shelves of bars outside Scotland.

An ideal way to demonstrate this difference in taste is used at whisky tasting sessions, where the participants are gently guided through a series of malts starting with the softer, fruity smelling ones and slowly working through to the stronger ones. With this manipulation of the palate, almost invariably the participants find the final dram the most appealing! As these participants do not always appreciate that the aim of tastings is to show how good even the stronger malts are when the palate has been tutored, they are liable to seek out the strongest one to try again at a later date, only to find it tastes too strong – their palate has not really developed sufficiently to cope with it without more experience. So how should a palate be developed?

It is perhaps advisable to start with a whisky mix, as long as the whisky is a blend, or a grain such as Invergordon, and not a malt. Lemonade, soda, even water and ice are possible mixes for blended whisky. This will begin to train the senses and on cold days a Whisky Mac (blended whisky and Green Ginger) will provide a feeling of warmth that goes hand in hand with other pleasant sensations. A really fine blend — such as Black Bottle — can then be attempted neat.

Graduation to a malt requires good company and careful thought. For most beginners the spirit should not assail the taste buds, but inveigle the senses through an appealing scent, subtle taste and soothing after effects. The aroma, which should be savoured before a sip is taken, can be spicy, fruity, flowery or peaty, and as with other scents like perfume and aftershave, individual preferences must be considered. The taste for the inexperienced should not be fierce — instead, the malt should be chosen from among the smooth, velvety and honeyed selections. Some are dry and others a little sweet, and once again personal preference must be recognized.

After effects are every bit as important, as the palate can be attacked some time after a stronger malt has been imbibed, and this can be unpleasant to the unwary. There are a variety of exciting after-effects that should be experienced and appreciated. The sparkles on the tongue and roof of the mouth provided by such malts as Oban and Aberlour are quite delightful, the feeling of being massaged, not just in the mouth but all over the shoulders and back, as produced by such as Glendullan after only one sip will help to cure most stress reactions. There are sensations of glowing warmth in the mouth, further reminiscent tastes of fruit or other pleasant foods and even a very delayed sharpness that comes as an unexpected surprise.

The use of miniatures is extremely helpful in identifying whiskies that appeal most to an individual. Further tutoring of the palate should be by experiencing the stronger ones in graduated steps, rather than by assaulting an unprepared and unsuspecting mouth!

Very simply, to drink a malt whisky properly, in order to obtain maximum enjoyment, it is necessary to consider the smell, taste and after-effects that would appeal to a particular individual. Time should be spent appreciating the aroma, taking only a small sip, letting it roll around the mouth before swallowing it and then awaiting the enjoyment of its after-effects. It is also well to remember that mood and the time of day as well as the weather conditions play a role in palate appeal. What may at the end of a horrible day seem like the most wonderful malt on earth, could well appear boring and inadequate on a cold winter's night or overwhelming in the middle of a happy gathering on a glorious summer's afternoon. Remember, too, that a palate will change with experience.

There are many, many blends, a few grain whiskies, a number of vatted malts and about 160 single malts (from approximately 120 distilleries, with some producing more than one year and volume) from which to choose. All are different, each with a different effect on different palates and providing the customer with a wonderful choice and opportunity to learn about a fascinating topic. If the beginner treats whisky with respect, the experiences encountered in the process of development will prove enchanting.

Taste rating

The discussions on the different whiskies which follow contain a Taste Rating of 1–5. This is not intended to be a judgement on the quality or relative standard of the spirit, nor is it possible to place strength and flavour together satisfactorily. Rather, it can be used as an indicator of accessibility of the whisky for a relatively inexperienced palate. A whisky may be mild or strong and still either lack flavour or exude it, so this rating concerns the degree of flavour, while at the same time allowing for the strength interfering with a person's ability to appreciate the flavour. The basic categories are as follows:

1 — Popular with particular palates; spirituous, with a very mild flavour

2 — Good for beginners; appealing taste and flavour for most palates at certain times

2-3 — Also good for beginners, but a little stronger than 2. One to return to again and again

3 — A dram for everyone; not too powerful, with pleasant sensations

3-4 — This should also appeal to most tastes, but is slightly stronger, so the palate requires a little more experience

4 — Very pleasing; a stronger spirit, ideal for those with more experience

5 — Robust; only for the well developed palate

HIGHLAND
SINGLE MALT
SCOTCH WHISKY

ABERFELDY

Aberfeldy Distillery, Aberfeldy, Perthshire

TYPE Single malt

BOTTLING AGE 15 years

STRENGTH 43%

TASTE RATING 3

MINIATURES Yes

COMMENTS Basically a dry malt with a medium body and clean, fresh character, but with a distinctly peaty background.

DISTILLERY Aberfeldy Distillery stands near the River Tay, at the town from which it takes its name. Building began in 1896 and the distillery opened two years later. It was built by Dewar's but is now owned by United Distillers, and almost all of its production goes into blends.

VISITORS Visitors are welcome 0930–1630 Mon.–Fri. (times are restricted in winter). Telephone 0887-820330.

ABERLOUR

Aberlour-Glenlivet Distillery,
Aberlour, Banffshire

TYPE Single malt

BOTTLING AGE 10, 12 years

STRENGTH 40%, 43%

TASTE RATING 3

MINIATURES Yes

COMMENTS A smooth, rich, sherried Speyside malt which is an ideal after-dinner drink.

DISTILLERY Established in the 1860s, Aberlour Distillery was rebuilt in the early 1880s after its destruction in a fire. It sits below Ben Rinnes from whose slopes it draws its water, said to be an important characteristic of its distinctive flavour. In the distillery grounds is the well of St Drostan (or Dunstan), the tenth-century missionary and patron saint of Aberlour who later became Archbishop of Canterbury. Since its acquisition by the Pernod Ricard company in 1974, Aberlour has become one of the most popular whiskies in France.

VISITORS Visitors are welcome by appointment. Telephone 0340-871204 to arrange.

64

AN CNOC

Knockdhu Distillery, Knock, Banffshire

TYPE Single malt

BOTTLING AGE 12 years

STRENGTH 40%

TASTE RATING 2–3

MINIATURES Yes

COMMENTS An Cnoc's dryish aroma is complemented by a mellow sweetness in the flavor. This Highland malt was previously known as Knockdhu.

DISTILLERY Knockdhu Distillery was established in 1893 on a favored site: with water available from Knock Hill, barley from the nearby farmlands, and a good supply of local peat. Although both buildings and machinery have since been modified, the production process remains essentially the same, with the two originally designed pot stills remaining. The distillery is owned by Inver House.

VISITORS The distillery is not open to visitors.

THE ANTIQUARY

United Distillers, Kilmarnock, Ayrshire

TYPE De luxe blend

BOTTLING AGE 0, 12 years

STRENGTH 40%

TASTE RATING 3

MINIATURES No

COMMENTS A smooth, well-balanced, premium blend which displays the mellowness expected from its blend of whiskies.

BLENDERS Now owned by United Distillers, Sanderson is the producer of The Antiquary. It was one of the blending companies begun in the early–mid nineteenth century which were responsible for the popularizing of blended whiskies in the lucrative markets of southern England. Sanderson was also a founder of the North British Distillery company in 1885, ensuring supplies of good grain whisky for his blends.

ARDBEG

Ardbeg Distillery, Port Ellen,
Islay, Argyllshire

TYPE Single Malt

BOTTLING AGE Varies

STRENGTH Varies

TASTE RATING 5

MINIATURES Yes

COMMENTS With a dominant aroma and insistent peatiness, Ardbeg's flavour is balanced by sweeter tones. Considered the most pungent of all Scotch whiskies, it is available from independent bottlers.

DISTILLERY The distillery was opened in 1815, one of several established near the sea in an area which was originally used by smugglers. It was bought by Hiram Walker in the 1950s, primarily to use its produce in blending; blenders use Islay malts in the way that a chef might use a strong flavour like garlic. Nearby Lochs Uigeadale and Arinambeast supply the water which, together with local peat, produces a distinctively Islay malt. Ardbeg is operated by Allied Distillers.

VISITORS The distillery is not suitable for visitors.

ARDMORE

Ardmore Distillery, Kennethmont, Aberdeenshire

TYPE Single malt

BOTTLING AGE Varies

STRENGTH Varies

TASTE RATING 4

MINIATURES Yes

COMMENTS A full-bodied Speyside malt which is both robust and sweet. An ideal after-dinner dram, although it is not easy to come by; available as a single malt only through independent bottlers.

DISTILLERY The distillery at Ardmore was built by the Teacher family in 1898 and since that time almost all its production has gone into Teacher's blends. Today it is operated by Allied Distillers, so its product also features prominently in Allied's other blends. Although the distillery has been modernized, it still retains some of the original equipment, such as coal-fired stills, used in the production of whisky at the end of the last century.

VISITORS Visitors are welcome by appointment. Telephone 04643-213 to arrange.

PRODUCT OF SCOTLAND

DISTILLED
1977
—SINGLE—
HIGHLAND

ARDMORE

70cl   40%
                        VOL

Trademark of Proprietors:
Wm. Teacher & Sons Ltd
—MALT—
SCOTCH
WHISKY

SPECIALLY SELECTED, PRODUCED & BOTTLED
BY & UNDER THE RESPONSIBILITY OF
GORDON & MACPHAIL, ELGIN, SCOTLAND
MALT BOTTLING

Established 1842

CADENHEAD'S

AUTHENTIC
COLLECTION

150th anniversary bottling
Single Malt Scotch Whisky

This whisky has been bottled from a selected individual cask.
In its natural state and shows the character of that cask.
It has not been diluted with water. It has not been treated to
change its colour and is free from all additives. It has
not been subjected to any filtration that might remove
natural constituents and spoil its flavour.
It is the authentic product of its distillery.

Bottled by Wm. Cadenhead, 32 Union Street, Campbeltown,
SCOTLAND

From
ARDMORE
Distillery

Distilled December 1978 and bottled March 1992
Matured in an oak cask
for 13 years
Product of Scotland

70cl   61.1% vol

AUCHENTOSHAN

Auchentoshan Distillery, Dalmuir, Dunbartonshire

TYPE Single malt

BOTTLING AGE 10, 21 years

STRENGTH 40%, 43%

TASTE RATING 2–3

MINIATURES Yes

COMMENTS A light, sweetish whisky whose smooth qualities are perhaps partially owed to the process of triple, rather than the more common double distillation.

DISTILLERY Although Auchentoshan Distillery lies south of the Highland Line (the line initiated by the Customs and Excise to differentiate area boundaries between styles of whisky), it uses peat and water from north of the line, so theoretically could be said to have a foot in both camps. It is, however, officially recognized as a Lowland distillery and whisky. Founded in the early nineteenth century, part of its interesting history includes surviving bombing in the Clydebank Blitz during the Second World War, when a stream of blazing whisky was said to have flowed from the building.

VISITORS Visitors are welcome by appointment. Telephone 03897-8561 to arrange.

AULTMORE

*Aultmore Distillery, Aultmore,
Keith, Banffshire*

TYPE Single malt

BOTTLING AGE 12 years

STRENGTH 43%

TASTE RATING 3

MINIATURES Yes

COMMENTS A faintly peaty aroma leads into this smooth, fruity, well-balanced whisky which has become deservedly better known in recent years.

DISTILLERY Aultmore Distillery was established in 1895 at the tail end of the whisky boom by the owner of Benrinnes Distillery. The area, with its abundant peat and water supplies, was infamous in the past for illicit distilling. Peat used in the production process is taken from a nearby moss, and the water is taken from local springs. The distillery passed to Dewars in 1923, and was improved and upgraded in the 1970s. It is now owned by United Distillers.

VISITORS The distillery is open to visitors by appointment only. Telephone 05422-2762.

BALBLAIR

Balblair Distillery, Edderton, Tain, Ross-shire

TYPE Single malt

BOTTLING AGE 10 years

STRENGTH 40%

TASTE RATING 3

MINIATURES Yes

COMMENTS A distinctive Highland malt whose slightly dry sharpness is nicely balanced by a light note of sweetness. Good as an aperitif, it is available from independent bottlers.

DISTILLERY Although its origins are lost in the mists of illicit distillation, it is claimed that Balblair was founded in 1749, which would make it one of the oldest distilleries in the country. It is set in pretty countryside in an area known as the 'parish of peats'. The present buildings date from the 1870s and are owned by Allied Distillers.

VISITORS The distillery has no reception centre, but visitors are welcome by appointment. Telephone 086282-273 to arrange.

BALLANTINE'S FINEST

Allied Distillers, Dumbarton, Dunbartonshire

TYPE Blend

STRENGTH 40%, 43%

TASTE RATING 2–3

MINIATURES Yes

COMMENTS Ballantine's Finest is, like the company's
other blends, characteristically mellow and well-rounded
with a soft, unassertive peaty flavour. Their range of
blends also includes Ballantine's Gold Seal 12-year-old,
Ballantine's 17 Years Old and Ballantine's 30-year-old,
considered to be the oldest (and most expensive) blend
available.

BLENDERS Ballantine is owned by the Hiram Walker
Group and operated by their subsidiary, Allied Distillers.
Hiram Walker first moved into the Scotch whisky market in the 1930s, extending their interests to blending by
the acquisition of Ballantine in 1936. Glenburgie and
Miltonduff distilleries were bought the following year,
and their new, giant complex, with grain and malt distilleries, was operational in Dumbarton by 1938.

VISITORS The plant is not suitable for visitors.

BALMENACH

Balmenach Distillery, Cromdale, Moray

TYPE Single malt

BOTTLING AGE 12 years

STRENGTH 43%

TASTE RATING 4

MINIATURES Yes

COMMENTS A complicated, full-bodied malt best suited as an after-dinner dram.

SPEYSIDE
SINGLE MALT
SCOTCH WHISKY

Sometime in the early 19th, after walking in the *CROMDALE* hills with his 2 *BROTHERS*, *James M'Gregor* settled and established

BALMENACH

distillery. Spring water from beneath those same HILLS is still used to produce this RICH flavoured single MALT SCOTCH WHISKY of exemplary quality.

AGED 12 YEARS

43% vol   70cl

DISTILLERY The Balmenach Distillery, in the Haughs of Cromdale, is set in an area which was notorious for illicit distilling for many years before the Licensing Act of 1823. Built in 1824 by James McGregor (great-grandfather of Sir Robert Bruce Lockhart, author of the classic 1951 book, *Scotch*), Balmenach was one of the first distilleries in the Highlands to be licensed under the 1823 act. Most of its production today goes into United Distillers' blends. In 1993 this distillery was earmarked for closure by United Distillers.

VISITORS Visitors are welcome by appointment, 0930–1600. Telephone 0479-2569 to arrange.

THE BALVENIE

Balvenie Distillery, Dufftown, Keith, Banffshire

SINGLE MALT

HIGHLAND MALT   SCOTCH WHISKY

The Balvenie

Founder's Reserve

70cl   *Established 1892*   40% Vol

TYPE   Single malt

BOTTLING AGE   10 years (Founder's Reserve),
                 8 years (Classic)

STRENGTH   40%, 43%

TASTE RATING   3

MINIATURES   Yes

COMMENTS   Founder's Reserve is mellow malt with a
complementary dry note to its sweet, honeyed tones.
The more expensive Classic, difficult to obtain in the
UK, spends its final year maturing in oloroso (sweet)
sherry casks which impart to it a distinctive darker colour
and richer flavour.

THE BALVENIE cont.

DISTILLERY Built in 1892 near the ruins of fourteenth-century Balvenie Castle by the Grants of Glenfiddich who already owned its now-famous parent distillery nearby on the banks of the River Fiddich. Balvenie Distillery still has a traditional hand-turned malting floor and grows its own barley, which is also used in the production of Glenfiddich. Both distilleries also draw their water from the Robbie Dubh Burn, yet their respective products taste quite different.

VISITORS The distillery is not open to visitors.

BANFF

Banff Distillery, Banff, Banffshire

TYPE Single malt

BOTTLING AGE Varies

STRENGTH Varies

TASTE RATING 2—3

MINIATURES Yes

COMMENTS A pleasant, slightly smoky, sweet bouquet leads into a whisky with a rather assertive taste.

A rare malt, available from independent merchants only.

DISTILLERY This distillery had an eventful history after its founding in 1863. It survived damage by fire in the 1870s, and was one of the few distilleries to be bombed during the Second World War, when thousands of gallons of whisky had to be thrown away to prevent the spread of fire. It was reported that the whisky running over the land and into nearby streams caused intoxication among the local farm animals and birds, and that dairy cows could not stand up to be milked! The distillery also once supplied whisky to Parliament. It was closed down by its parent company, the Distillers Company Ltd, in 1983, and has since been demolished.

BELL'S EXTRA SPECIAL

United Distillers, East Mains, Broxburn, West Lothian

TYPE Blend

STRENGTH 40%

TASTE RATING 2–3

MINIATURES Yes

COMMENTS The most popular blend in the UK, Bell's Extra Special is a pleasant, medium-bodied whisky with a nutty aroma and a spicy flavour.

BLENDERS The merchants and blending company which ultimately became Arthur Bell & Sons was begun in Perth in 1825. Bell himself joined the firm as a traveller in the 1840s and became a partner in 1851. The 'Extra Special' name, accompanied by Bell's signature, was registered as a trade mark in 1895. Large-scale expansion came in the 1930s after the ending of Prohibition in the USA, when Bell's acquired three of the company's subsequent complement of five distilleries: Blair Athol, Dufftown-Glenlivet and Inchgower. Pittyvaich-Glenlivet was built in 1975, and Bladnoch bought in 1983. Bell's blend is now owned by United Distillers.

BENRIACH

Benriach Distillery, Elgin, Moray

CONNOISSEURS CHOICE

Connoisseurs Choice, a range of single malts from various districts of Scotland

The distilleries situated in the area of the valley of the River Spey produce some of the finest malt whiskies

GRAMPIANS

SINGLE SPEYSIDE
MALT SCOTCH WHISKY
DISTILLED AT
BENRIACH
DISTILLERY
PROPRIETORS The Longmorn-Glenlivet Distilleries Ltd

DISTILLED **1982** DISTILLED

SPECIALLY SELECTED, PRODUCED AND BOTTLED BY
GORDON & MACPHAIL
ELGIN SCOTLAND
PRODUCT OF SCOTLAND

70cl   40%vol

TYPE Single malt

BOTTLING AGE Varies

STRENGTH Varies

TASTE RATING 4

MINIATURES Yes

COMMENTS A medium-bodied whisky with malty overtones and a rich, sweetish finish. When available, it is through independent merchants' bottlings.

DISTILLERY Originally built in the 1890s, Benriach was closed in 1900, after recession hit the previously booming whisky industry. It was refitted and reopened in 1965, although not completely modernized, still retaining its hand-turned malting floor. The company is owned by Seagram, and most of its produce goes into their blends.

VISITORS The distillery is not open to visitors.

BENRINNES

Benrinnes Distillery, Aberlour, Banffshire

TYPE Single Malt

BOTTLING AGE 15 years

STRENGTH 43%

TASTE RATING 4

MINIATURES Yes

COMMENTS This is a complex Speyside malt which has hints of wood and grass to its flavour, and a fruity aftertaste.

DISTILLERY Built almost 700 feet up the slopes of Ben Rinnes, from which it takes its name, this distillery is believed to have been founded in 1835 although evidence exists of distilling on this site in 1826. It was largely rebuilt and modernized in the 1950s. Most of its production is distilled three times rather than the more usual twice, and almost all is used in United Distillers' blends.

VISITORS The distillery is open to visitors by appointment only. Telephone 0340-871215.

SPEYSIDE
SINGLE MALT
SCOTCH WHISKY

BENRINNES

distillery stands on the northern shoulder of BEN RINNES 700 feet above sea level. It is ideally located to exploit the natural advantages of the area-pure air, peat and barley and the finest of hill water, which rises through granite from springs on the summit of the mountain. The resulting single MALT SCOTCH WHISKY, is rounded and mellow.

AGED 15 YEARS

Distilled & Bottled in SCOTLAND
BENRINNES DISTILLERY
Aberlour, Banffshire, Scotland.

43% vol 70 cl

BENROMACH

Benromach Distillery, Forres, Moray

PURE MALT SCOTCH WHISKY
from

Benromach
Distillery

Proprietors: J. & W. Hardie Ltd.

75 cl   Bottled by Wm. Cadenhead,
             18 Golden Square, Aberdeen   45% vol
             Scotland

TYPE Single malt

BOTTLING AGE Varies

STRENGTH Varies

TASTE RATING 2–3

MINIATURES Yes

COMMENTS Subtle and sweet, this Speyside malt has a gentle, fragrant palate and refreshing aftertaste. It is available from independent merchants.

DISTILLERY Benromach was built just outside Forres in 1898, in the years of expansion for the whisky industry, and it underwent extensive reconstruction in 1966 and 1974. Supplies of the whisky may not be easy to come by, as the distillery has been closed since 1983, and much of the remaining stock goes into most United Distillers blends. The distillery was sold by United Distillers in 1992.

BERRY'S ALL MALT

Berry Brothers and Rudd, London

TYPE Vatted malt

BOTTLING AGE 12 years

STRENGTH 40%

TASTE RATING 3–4

MINIATURES Yes

COMMENTS Robust in
character with a medium-
to-full body, Berry's All
Malt has a lightly seaweedy
nose with spicy and smoky flavours.

BLENDERS Berry Brothers and Rudd have been successful London vintners since the seventeenth century.
Their main product in the whisky market is the famous
Cutty Sark blend, one of the world's leading blends,
especially in the USA, Japan and Europe. Berry Brothers
and Rudd have other interests in blending, including
Cutty 12, a 12-year-old blend produced for UK and
foreign markets.

BIG "T"

Tomatin Distillery Company,
Tomatin, Inverness-shire

TYPE Blend and De luxe

BOTTLING AGE 5 years
minimum (standard blend),
12 years (de luxe)

STRENGTH 40%, 43%

TASTE RATING
  1 (standard blend),
  2 (de luxe)

MINIATURES Yes
  (standard blend only)

COMMENTS Big "T" standard blend is a whisky of light-to-medium body with a fresh, malty sweetness, well-balanced by a hint of peat. The 12-year-old de luxe is an extremely smooth blend, most of which is reserved for export.

BLENDERS The Tomatin Distillery Company's premises is the largest-capacity distillery in the country, with production as high as five million gallons per annum. The company declined in the 1980s and went into receivership, but was bought by the Japanese firms of Takara Schuzo and Okura, thus becoming the first

Scotch whisky distillery to be acquired by Japanese owners.

VISITORS Visitors can visit the malt whisky distillery; see Tomatin entry for details.

TYPE Blend

STRENGTH 40%

TASTE RATING 2

MINIATURES Yes

COMMENTS A clean, pleasantly mild whisky, Black & White has a fresh, grassy flavour which is complemented by a light sweetness.

BLENDERS Black & White is the standard blend of the company begun in 1884 by James Buchanan as a whisky blenders and merchants in London. Within a year it was a success, with a contract to supply the House of Commons, and the firm was one of the prime movers in the successful introduction of blended whiskies to the English market. The whisky was bottled and labelled in a very distinctive black and white livery, and this popular nickname eventually was adopted as the brand name. The company amalgamated with Dewars in 1915, and both joined the Distillers Company ten years later. Black & White is currently available only in markets outside the UK.

BLACK BOTTLE

Allied Distillers, Dumbarton, Dunbartonshire

TYPE Blend

STRENGTH 40%

TASTE RATING 2–3

MINIATURES Yes

COMMENTS Black Bottle is a smooth, superior-quality blend with a fresh hint of peat, complemented by sweeter, malty notes.

BLENDERS Black Bottle was first produced by a family of merchants from Aberdeen in 1879, and has been a premium blend since its first appearance. The company was sold to Long John in 1959, and was acquired by Allied Distillers in 1990. The distinctive pot-still-shaped bottle rapidly became its trademark, and has remained virtually unchanged to the present day.

VISITORS The plant is not suitable for visitors.

BLADNOCH

Bladnoch Distillery, Bladnoch,
Wigtown, Wigtownshire

TYPE Single malt

BOTTLING AGE 10 years

STRENGTH 43%

TASTE RATING 3

MINIATURES Yes

COMMENTS Bladnoch is a
light-to-medium-bodied
malt with a light, fragrant,
lemony aroma and a gentle,
unassertive flavour with fruity tones.

DISTILLERY Bladnoch is Scotland's most southerly distillery, in Wigtownshire, and is also one of its oldest. It
was built in 1817 and stands on the banks of the River
Bladnoch, in the village of the same name. It has had
many owners this century and has been closed twice,
but has enjoyed a new lease of life under the ownership
of United Distillers. In 1993 this distillery was earmarked for closure by United Distillers.

VISITORS Visitors are welcome 1000–1600. Mon.–Fri.
Larger groups should telephone in advance. Telephone
09884-2235.

BLAIR ATHOL

Blair Athol Distillery, Pitlochry, Perthshire

TYPE Single malt

BOTTLING AGE 12 years

STRENGTH 43%

TASTE RATING 2–3

MINIATURES Yes

COMMENTS Blair Athol is a light, fresh single malt with dry notes and a hint of smokiness.

DISTILLERY This is a picturesquely sited distillery on a wooded hillside on the outskirts of the tourist centre of Pitlochry. Blair Athol is unusual in that it is twelve miles distant from the village after which it is named. Established in 1825, the distillery was bought by Bell's in 1933 and sympathetically upgraded. It is now owned by United Distillers. Its water comes from the Allt Dour (Burn of the Otter) which flows past the distillery en route to the River Tummel.

VISITORS Visitors are welcome 0930–1700 Mon.–Sat. all year, and 1200–1700 Sun., Easter–Oct. Telephone 0796-472234 to arrange.

BOWMORE

Bowmore Distillery, Bowmore, Islay, Argyllshire

TYPE Single malt

BOTTLING AGE 10, 12, 17, 21, 25 years

STRENGTH 40%, 43%

TASTE RATING 3

MINIATURES Yes

COMMENTS With its pleasant aroma and peaty–fruity flavour, Bowmore is a good Islay malt for newcomers to these distinctive whiskies to try.

DISTILLERY Established in the 1770s, Bowmore is reputed to be the oldest legal distillery on Islay. It stands in the island's main town and overlooks Loch Indaal, and its water is taken from the peaty River Laggan. The distillery has been a thriving concern since its acquisition in 1963 by Stanley P. Morrison of Glasgow.

VISITORS Visitors are welcome by appointment. Telephone 049681-671 to arrange.

BRUICHLADDICH

Bruichladdich Distillery,
Bruichladdich, Islay, Argyllshire

TYPE Single malt

BOTTLING AGE 10 years

STRENGTH 40%

TASTE RATING 3

MINIATURES Yes

COMMENTS A subtle malt,
and less medicinal in its
flavour than other Islay
whiskies, Bruichladdich is
a lightish, dry, fresh-
tasting whisky.

PRODUCT OF SCOTLAND

BRUICHLADDICH
ISLAY

AGED 10 YEARS

SINGLE MALT
SCOTCH WHISKY

DISTILLED AND BOTTLED BY
BRUICHLADDICH DISTILLERY CO. LTD.
BRUICHLADDICH ISLE OF ISLAY

Founded 1881

70cl   Bottled in Scotland   40% vol

VISITORS Built in 1881, Bruichladdich is Scotland's
most westerly distillery. Its water comes from an inland
reservoir and, unlike the other distilleries, is not drawn
from springs which have flowed over peaty land; this
has been suggested as a reason why its peaty flavour is less
intense than other Islay malts.

VISITORS Visitors are welcome by appointment.
Telephone 049685-221 to arrange.

BUNNAHABHAIN

Bunnahabhain Distillery,
Port Askaig, Islay, Argyllshire

TYPE Single malt

BOTTLING AGE 12 years

STRENGTH 40%

TASTE RATING 3

MINIATURES Yes

COMMENTS Less characteristically peaty than some other Islay malts, Bunnahabhain is a mellow whisky with an aromatic flavour.

DISTILLERY Bunnahabhain, on the north of Islay, is one of the more isolated of the island's distilleries. Founded in 1881, it was owned by the Islay Distillery Company who bought Glen Rothes Distillery in 1887, forming the Highland Distilleries Company. They still own Bunnahabhain Distillery today.

VISITORS Visitors are welcome by appointment. Telephone 049684-646 to arrange.

CAOL ILA

Caol Ila Distillery,
Port Askaig, Islay, Argyllshire

ISLAY
SINGLE MALT *SCOTCH WHISKY*

CAOL ILA

*distillery, built in 1846 is situated near Port Askaig on the Isle of Islay.
Steamers used to call twice a week to collect whisky from this remote
site in a cove facing the Isle of Jura. Water supplies for mashing
come from Loch nam Ban although the sea provides water for
condensing. Unusual for an Islay this single MALT SCOTCH
WHISKY has a fresh aroma and a light yet well rounded flavour*

AGED **15** YEARS

43% vol *Distilled & bottled in SCOTLAND. CAOL ILA DISTILLERY, Port Askaig, Isle of Islay, Scotland* 70cl

TYPE Single malt

BOTTLING AGE 15 years

STRENGTH 43%

TASTE RATING 4

MINIATURES Yes

COMMENTS Nicely balanced Caol Ila is not the peatiest of the Islay whiskies, but is pleasantly dry with a well-rounded body.

DISTILLERY Caol Ila was established in 1846 and overlooks the Sound of Islay (which is also the English translation of its name). It previously used its own wharf for the despatching of its product. The distillery has been rebuilt twice, at almost 100-year intervals, in 1879 and 1972. The most recent modernization almost doubled the distillery's output. Caol Ila is now owned by United Distillers.

VISITORS Visitors are welcome Mon.–Fri. by appointment. Telephone 049684-207 to arrange.

CAPERDONICH

Caperdonich Distillery, Rothes, Moray

TYPE Single malt

BOTTLING AGE Varies

STRENGTH Varies

TASTE RATING 3

MINIATURES Yes

COMMENTS A pleasant Speyside malt of light-to-medium body, with a delicately fruity flavour combined with a hint of peat.

DISTILLERY Originally owned by J & J Grant, this distillery was built across the road from their main production centre at Glen Grant. The two distilleries were to be treated as one for licensing purposes, so a pipe spanned the road to carry the produce of Caperdonich (then known as Glen Grant Number Two) across for blending. Built to take advantage of the boom years of the 1890s, it suffered with the fall-off in consumption and was closed in the early 1900s, waiting over sixty years for renovation and reopening under the new name of Caperdonich. Most of its produce goes into blends, with only some available from independent merchants.

VISITORS The distillery is not open to visitors.

CARDHU

Cardhu Distillery, Knockando, Moray

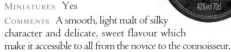

TYPE Single malt

BOTTLING AGE 12 years

STRENGTH 40%

TASTE RATING 2–3

MINIATURES Yes

COMMENTS A smooth, light malt of silky character and delicate, sweet flavour which make it accessible to all from the novice to the connoisseur.

DISTILLERY Whisky distilling had been carried on illegally in this area for a long time before Cardow Distillery, as it was then, was founded and licensed in 1824. The distillery was bought by John Walker of Kilmarnock during the boom years of the 1890s, producing a vatted and a single malt under the Cardhu name. It was modernized in 1965 and its single malt was relaunched, with the distillery name being changed in 1981 to match that of its product. It is now owned by United Distillers. Cardhu enjoys a splendid situation overlooking the Spey valley and has recently been refurbished.

VISITORS The distillery is on the Whisky Trail and visitors are welcome 0930–1630 Mon.–Fri. all year, and 0930–1630 Sat., May–Sept. Telephone 03406-204/439.

CHIVAS REGAL

Chivas Brothers, Paisley

TYPE De luxe

BOTTLING AGE 12 years

STRENGTH 40%, 43%

TASTE RATING 2–3

MINIATURES Yes

COMMENTS Chivas Regal is a high-quality de luxe blend of mature malt whiskies; the result is a smooth, mellow whisky with a malty sweetness and a trace of peatiness.

BLENDERS Chivas Brothers is a subsidiary of the Canadian drinks firm Seagram, by whom it was bought in 1949. The origins of the Chivas Brothers company can be traced back to the establishment of a wine and spirit merchant and licensed grocer in Aberdeen in 1801. Owning nine malt distilleries, Seagram is an important company in the Scotch whisky market. Chivas Regal is one of several Seagram blends which include Passport, 100 Pipers and the premium 21-year-old Royal Salute.

CHOICE OLD CAMERON BRIG

Cameronbridge Distillery, Cameron Bridge, Fife

TYPE Grain

STRENGTH 40%

TASTE RATING 1

MINIATURES Yes

COMMENTS Like other grain whiskies, a lighter spirit than malt, with a fresh taste and an element of smoothness.

Specially Selected Choice Old
Cameron Brig
SCOTCH WHISKY

JOHN HAIG & CO DISTILLERS
CAMERON BRIDGE DISTILLERY
THE KINGDOM OF FIFE
SCOTLAND

40% vol   70cl

DISTILLERY Cameronbridge had been operating for several years before it was acquired in 1824 by John Haig, and produced both grain and malt whisky using a mixture of pot and patent stills until 1929 before concentrating on grain alone. Haig's company were among the founders of the Distillers Company in 1877, and United Distillers still own the distillery today.

VISITORS The distillery is not open to visitors.

THE CLAYMORE

Whyte & Mackay, Glasgow

TYPE Blend

STRENGTH 40%

TASTE RATING 2–3

MINIATURES Yes

COMMENTS A nicely rounded, medium-bodied blend with a mellow aroma and a well-balanced, smooth and rich taste.

PRODUCERS The Claymore is a popular blend which is owned by Whyte & Mackay, the blending and bottling company begun in 1882. As with many of the company's whiskies, The Claymore is popular in export markets as well as in the UK, where it is among the top five best-selling blends.

VISITORS The blending and bottling plant is not open to visitors.

CLYNELISH

Clynelish Distillery, Brora, Sutherland

TYPE Single malt

BOTTLING AGE 14 years

STRENGTH 43%

TASTE RATING 3

MINIATURES Yes

COMMENTS A medium-bodied, full-flavoured whisky with many devotees. It is slightly dry to the taste, with a hint of peat.

DISTILLERY The distillery had its origins in the early years of the nineteenth century and was built by a future Duke of Sutherland to take advantage of the cheap grain grown on the coastal farms of his tenants. It was bought by Ainslie and Heilbron in 1896. A new distillery was built on adjacent land in 1967–68, taking the name Clynelish, while the original distillery, now renamed Brora, was closed by the Distillers Company Ltd, its parent company, in 1983. It is now owned by United Distillers.

VISITORS Visitors are welcome 0930–1630 Mon.–Fri. Telephone 0408-621444.

HIGHLAND
SINGLE MALT
SCOTCH WHISKY

One of the most northerly in Scotland,

CLYNELISH

distillery, was established in Brora by the Marquess of STAFFORD in 1819. Its building signalled the end of illicit distilling in the area and provided a ready market for locally grown barley. Water is piped from the CLYNEMILTON burn to produce this fruity, & slightly smoky single MALT SCOTCH WHISKY much appreciated by connoisseurs.

YEARS **14** OLD

43% vol   70 cl

Distilled & Bottled in SCOTLAND
CLYNELISH DISTILLERY
Brora, Sutherland, Scotland

COLEBURN

Coleburn Distillery,
Longmorn, Elgin, Moray

TYPE Single malt

BOTTLING AGE
Varies

STRENGTH Varies

TASTE RATING 3

MINIATURES Yes

COMMENTS A difficult-to-find malt with a delicate, fragrant aroma and pleasant, slightly flowery taste. Available bottled by independent merchants.

DISTILLERY Coleburn was built by John Robertson of Dundee in 1896 and was licensed to J & G Stewart, a subsidiary of the Distillers Company Ltd and blenders of Usher's whiskies. It was acquired by United Distillers and mothballed in 1985.

COLUMBA CREAM

John Murray & Co. (Mull), Calgary, Isle of Mull

TYPE Liqueur

BOTTLING AGE 4 years

STRENGTH 17%

TASTE RATING 2

MINIATURES Yes

COMMENTS A blend of four single malt whiskies, with the addition of honey and cream makes for a very pleasant and mellow whisky cream liqueur.

PRODUCERS John Murray have been producing Columba Cream for several years to a formula which is based on a traditional recipe. The company has offices on the Isle of Mull, and blending and bottling is currently carried out at their plant in Clydebank.

VISITORS The plant is not open to visitors.

CONVALMORE

Convalmore Distillery, Dufftown,
Keith, Banffshire

TYPE Single malt

BOTTLING AGE Varies

STRENGTH Varies

TASTE RATING 3

MINIATURES Yes

COMMENTS Available from independent merchants, this is a dry, aromatic, atypical Speyside malt which works best as a digestif.

DISTILLERY W P Lowrie, the present licensed distillers, bought Convalmore in 1904, eleven years after its founding. Considerably damaged by fire in 1909, it was rebuilt in 1910 when experiments were made in the production of malt whisky from patent stills; this was abandoned in 1916, however, in favour of the traditional pot-still method which was considered to mature the whisky better. Almost all the production of Convalmore goes into blends. The distillery was acquired by United Distillers and was mothballed in 1985.

CRAGGANMORE

Cragganmore Distillery, Ballindalloch, Banffshire

TYPE Single malt

BOTTLING AGE 12 years

STRENGTH 40%

TASTE RATING 3–4

MINIATURES Yes

COMMENTS A Speyside
malt of distinctive and
complex character,
Cragganmore has a deli-
cate aroma and smoky finish.

DISTILLERY The first distillery to be built alongside an
existing railway, Cragganmore was built in 1869 and
took its name from nearby Craggan More Hill. It was
built by John Smith (a man of great bulk, also known
locally as 'Cragganmore') and is now licensed to D & J
McCallum. Most of its production goes into blends,
especially Old Parr, and until a few years ago, the single
malt was only infrequently available. The distillery is
owned by United Distillers.

VISITORS The distillery is not open to visitors.

CRAIGELLACHIE

Craigellachie Distillery, Craigellachie, Aberlour, Banffshire

TYPE Single malt

BOTTLING AGE 14 years

STRENGTH 43%

TASTE RATING 3

MINIATURES Yes

COMMENTS A smoky-smelling and tasting malt of medium body, Craigellachie works well as an after-dinner dram. Available from independent whisky merchants only.

DISTILLERY This distillery is pleasantly situated on high ground above the River Spey outside Dufftown. It was built in 1891 by the Craigellachie Distillery Co., a founder of which was Peter Mackie, the creator of the White Horse brand. Mackie and Co. (later White Horse Distillers) subsequently bought the distillery in 1915. It is now owned by United Distillers and most of its production is devoted to blending.

VISITORS The distillery is not open to visitors.

CRAWFORD'S THREE STAR

Whyte & Mackay, Glasgow

TYPE Blend

STRENGTH 40%

TASTE RATING 2

MINIATURES Yes

COMMENTS A smooth, nicely balanced blend with light, malty flavours. The de luxe Five Star is a richer whisky with mild sherried hints.

BLENDERS A & A Crawford was established as a whisky merchant and blenders in Leith in 1860. Although the original founders died before the end of the century, the business was taken over by their sons who were responsible for the launching of the successful Crawford's Three Star blend at the start of the century. The de luxe Five Star appeared in the 1920s and was also well received. The company was acquired by the Distillers Company Ltd in 1944 and ownership subsequently passed to Whyte and Mackay in 1986.

TRADE MARK

ESTD. 1860

CRAWFORD'S

★ ★ ★

SPECIAL RESERVE
OLD SCOTCH WHISKY

DISTILLED, BLENDED AND BOTTLED IN SCOTLAND.

A.A.Crawford tb

A.A. CRAWFORD & CO. GLASGOW G2 5RG, SCOTLAND.

70 cl ℮   40% Vol.

ESTD.   1860

YEARS **12** OLD

CRAWFORD'S
FIVE STAR

★ ★ ★ ★ ★

DELUXE
SCOTCH WHISKY

A.A.Crawford tb

DISTILLED, BLENDED AND BOTTLED IN SCOTLAND.
A.A. CRAWFORD & CO. GLASGOW G2 5RG, SCOTLAND.

70 cl   40% Vol.

CUTTY SARK

Berry Brothers and Rudd, London

TYPE Blend

STRENGTH 40%

TASTE RATING 2

MINIATURES Yes

COMMENTS A light, smooth whisky with a fresh, sweet flavour, Cutty Sark is one of the world's leading blends, especially in the USA, Japan and Europe.

BLENDERS The producers of Cutty Sark, Berry Brothers and Rudd, have been successful London vintners since the seventeenth century. Cutty Sark blend was launched in 1923 specifically for the American market, where it quickly became a brand leader, a position it has sustained ever since. The whisky's label was designed by the Scottish artist James McBey, who had an interest in maritime subjects, and it featured the nineteenth century clipper after which the whisky was named. A Scottish connection existed here, as the original Cutty Sark had been a character in the Burns poem, *Tam o' Shanter*. Berry Brothers and Rudd have other interests in blending, including Cutty 12, a 12-year-old blend produced for UK and foreign markets.

DAILUAINE

Dailuaine Distillery, Carron, Banffshire

SPEYSIDE
SINGLE MALT SCOTCH WHISKY

DAILUAINE

is the GAELIC for "the green vale". The *distillery*, established
in 1852, lies in a hollow by the *CARRON BURN* in *BANFFSHIRE*. This
single Malt Scotch Whisky has a *full bodied fruity nose* and a *smoky finish*.
For more than a hundred years all *distillery supplies* were despatched by
rail. The *steam locomotive* "DAILUAINE NO.1" was in use
from 1939 - 1967 and is preserved on the *STRATHSPEY RAILWAY*.

AGED **16** YEARS

43% vol   Distilled & Bottled in SCOTLAND. DAILUAINE DISTILLERY, Carron, Aberlour, Banffshire, Scotland   70 cl

TYPE Single malt

BOTTLING AGE 16 years

STRENGTH 43%

TASTE RATING 4

MINIATURES Yes

COMMENTS This is a rare malt, with a heathery and sweetish flavour.

DISTILLERY Dailuaine Distillery stands near the Spey below Ben Rinnes and was established in 1851 by William Mackenzie; it was subsequently taken over by his son, Thomas, and greatly expanded during the 1880s. It was one of a number of distilleries owned by the Dailuaine–Talisker Distillery Co., an amalgamated company formed by Mackenzie, but it is presently owned by United Distillers.

VISITORS The distillery is not open to visitors.

THE DALMORE

Dalmore Distillery, Alness, Ross-shire

TYPE Single malt

BOTTLING AGE 12 years

STRENGTH 40%

TASTE RATING 4

MINIATURES Yes

COMMENTS A smooth, full-bodied whisky with a hint of peat in its malted flavours. A good digestif.

DISTILLERY Built in 1839, Dalmore was bought in 1867 by the Mackenzie family, although ownership has now passed to Whyte & Mackay. The distillery is attractively set in a picturesque location with a wooded, hilly backdrop and outlook over the Cromarty Firth to the fertile Black Isle, a location which meant a break in the production of whisky during the First World War when the American navy took over the distillery and its access to the deepwater Cromarty Firth, for the manufacture of mines.

VISITORS Visitors are welcome by appointment at 1100 or 1400 Mon., Tue., Thur., early Sept.–mid June. Telephone 0349-882362 to arrange.

DALWHINNIE

*Dalwhinnie Distillery,
Dalwhinnie, Inverness-shire*

TYPE Single malt

BOTTLING AGE 15 years

STRENGTH 43%

TASTE RATING 2—3

MINIATURES Yes

COMMENTS Ideal as a pre- or post-dinner dram, Dalwhinnie is light and aromatic with a soft, heather-honey finish.

DISTILLERY Built in 1898 at the end of the boom years for the whisky industry, the distillery was known as Strathspey when it opened. It stands on the Drumochter Pass at a height of more than 1000 feet, close to pure water sources, and is Scotland's highest distillery. It is presently owned by United Distillers. Most of its output went to blending until 1988 when the single malt was developed.

VISITORS Visitors are welcome 0930–1700 Mon.–Fri. Telephone 05282-208/264.

DEANSTON

Deanston Distillery, Doune,
Stirlingshire

TYPE Single malt

BOTTLING AGE 12 years

STRENGTH 40%

TASTE RATING 3

MINIATURES Yes

COMMENTS A light, fresh, smooth Highland malt with a sweetish, fruity flavour.

DISTILLERY Originally a cotton mill dating from 1785, Deanston was converted to a whisky distillery in 1966. Although it stands on the banks of the River Teith, its water is brought from the nearby Trossachs. The Teith water is used, however, to generate electricity for the distillery. The mill's original weaving sheds, with their humidity control and their temperature, are perfect for maturing the whisky and are considered to add a natural smoothness to its character. Deanston was bought by Burn Stewart of Glasgow in 1991.

VISITORS The distillery is not open to visitors.

DEWAR'S WHITE LABEL

United Distillers, Inveralmond, Perthshire

TYPE Blend

STRENGTH 40%

TASTE RATING 2

MINIATURES Yes

COMMENTS Dewar's White Label, the best-selling Scotch whisky in the USA, has a slightly smoky aroma and a complex, delicate, malty flavour with a clean, dry finish.

BLENDERS John Dewar and Sons was one of the blending companies instrumental in the development of new whisky markets outside Scotland. Begun in Perth in 1846, it was the first company to sell its whisky in bottles as well as casks, thus opening up a new market in the home rather than just the licensed shop, pub or hotel. Dewar's was also a pioneer of whisky advertising and was one of the first companies whose bottles carried its company name. By the time it became part of the Distillers Company Ltd in 1925, it owned seven distilleries, two of which (Aberfeldy and Glen Ord) are still licensed to Dewar's. More than 90% of production is exported.

DIMPLE

*United Distillers, Banbeath,
Leven, Fife*

TYPE De luxe

BOTTLING AGE 15 years

STRENGTH 40%

TASTE RATING 2–3

MINIATURES Yes

COMMENTS Dimple, in its distinctive triangular bottle,
is a good quality de luxe blend which is also a leader in
its market in the UK. More sophisticated than the standard Haig blend, it has a mellow sweetness which is
harmoniously balanced by a smoky, peaty flavour.

BLENDERS Haig is a family name long associated with
the whisky industry, going back almost 350 years, when
Robert Haig, a farmer of Stirlingshire, was rebuked by
his local kirk session for distilling his whisky on a
Sunday. The Haigs were instrumental in introducing
new practices and machinery (for example the new patent
still in the 1830s) to the grain distilleries which they
built in Edinburgh and elsewhere in the east. The company was acquired by the Distillers Company Ltd in
1919 and today they hold the licence for three malt distilleries: Glenkinchie, Glenlossie and Mannochmore, as
well as Cameronbridge grain distillery in Fife.

DRAMBUIE

Drambuie, Kirkliston, West Lothian

TYPE Liqueur

STRENGTH 40%

TASTE RATING 2

MINIATURES Yes

COMMENTS Based on a blend of secret ingredients, Drambuie is a sweet after-dinner whisky liqueur with a rich and creamy honey-eyed flavour complemented by fragrant, fruity notes.

PRODUCERS Drambuie is produced in the Lothians, having moved from its original home on Skye at the start of this century after the decision was taken to produce the liqueur commercially. Drambuie ('the drink that satisfies') is chronicled as being the personal liqueur of Prince Charles Edward Stuart, Bonnie Prince Charlie. After his army's defeat by the Hanoverian army at Culloden in 1746, the prince fled to Skye with a few supporters. Among them was Captain John Mackinnon, a native of Skye, whom the prince rewarded for his loyalty by giving him his only remaining possession – the secret recipe for his personal liqueur.

VISITORS Welcome by appointment, 0930–1530 Mon.–Fri. Telephone 031-333 3531 to arrange.

DUFFTOWN

Dufftown-Glenlivet Distillery,
Dufftown, Keith, Banffshire

TYPE Single malt

BOTTLING AGE 15 years

STRENGTH 43%

TASTE RATING 2–3

MINIATURES Yes

COMMENTS A pleasant
Speyside malt with a delicate, fragrant aroma which is almost flowery, and a smooth, sweet taste. Doubles as a before- or after-dinner dram.

DISTILLERY Prettily situated at the water's edge in the Dullan Glen, this is one of seven distilleries in and around Dufftown, a major whisky production centre with plentiful resources of water, peat and, previously, barley. Despite the abundance of fresh water in the glen, there were disputes in the early years over water rights, some of which led to the nocturnal diversion and re-diversion of local supplies. The distillery finally gained the right to draw its supplies from Jock's Well, a reliable source of fine, sweet water some distance away.

VISITORS Visitors are welcome by appointment, 0900–1600. Larger parties should telephone in advance. Telephone 0340-20224 to arrange.

DUNKELD ATHOLL BROSE

Gordon and MacPhail,
Elgin, Moray

TYPE Liqueur

BOTTLING AGE 12 years

STRENGTH 35%

TASTE RATING 2

MINIATURES Yes

COMMENTS Based on a traditional recipe, this liqueur has a good whisky association coming through its sweetness. It is herbal on the nose, with a long, warming finish.

PRODUCERS Gordon and MacPhail started in business in 1895 as a licensed grocers and wine and spirit merchant. They have retained all the original aspects of their business as well as extending into vatting, blending and bottling, and they also produce this liqueur, which won a Silver Award (1985) at the International Wine and Spirit Competition and a Gold Award (1987), when it was named 'the best liqueur in the world'.

VISITORS Gordon and MacPhail's shop, South St, Elgin is open 0900–1715 Mon.–Wed. (0900–1300 Wed. in winter), 0830–1715 Thu.–Fri., 0900–1700 Sat.

THE EDRADOUR

Edradour Distillery, Pitlochry, Perthshire

TYPE Single malt

BOTTLING AGE 10 years

STRENGTH 40%

TASTE RATING 3

MINIATURES Yes

COMMENTS The Edradour is a
smooth Highland malt with
pleasant notes of fruit and malt
in its taste, complemented by a slight dryness.

BLENDERS Edradour is Scotland's smallest distillery, as
well as being one of its most picturesque. Built in 1837,
it stands on the steep banks of a burn in the Perthshire
countryside, and sympathetic modernization in 1982 left
its appearance unchanged. The distillery had been bought
by William Whiteley in 1933 and, despite a takeover in
1982 by Pernod Ricard subsidiary the House of
Campbell, Whiteley still hold the licence. Most of the
malt goes into their blends House of Lords and Clan
Campbell, and it is only since 1986 that The Edradour has
been available as a single malt under the distillery label.

VISITORS Visitors are welcome. Telephone 0796-
472095 to arrange.

THE FAMOUS GROUSE

Matthew Gloag and Son, Perth, Perthshire

TYPE Blend

STRENGTH 40%

TASTE RATING 2

MINIATURES Yes

COMMENTS The Famous Grouse is a light-to-medium-bodied whisky with a fresh smoothness and a pleasant, lightly peated flavour. It has been the most popular blend in Scotland for several years.

BLENDERS Matthew Gloag and Son began in Perth in 1800 as a licensed grocers, acquiring interests in blending and bottling as the firm expanded during the nineteenth century. What became their most famous product appeared at the end of the century, with the grouse on the name and label successfully capitalizing on the popularity of sporting pastimes among Victorian and Edwardian gentlemen. The company was bought by Highland Distilleries in 1970 and received the benefits of wider distribution and advertising. Highland Distilleries own Bunnahabhain, Glenglassaugh, Glen Rothes, Highland Park and Tamdhu-Glenlivet malt distilleries.

FRASER McDONALD

Gibson International, Glasgow

TYPE Blend

STRENGTH 40%

TASTE RATING 2–3

MINIATURES No

COMMENTS Fraser McDonald is a smooth and mellow blend whose light, fresh taste is underlain by gentle peaty notes.

BLENDERS Fraser McDonald is the standard blend of Gibson International, a company with widespread interests in the whisky industry, from distilling to exporting. The company was formed in 1988 to control, develop and promote their two distilleries (Glen Scotia and Littlemill) and associated blends. As well as its whiskies, Gibson International also has other interests in the spirits industry.

GLAYVA

Glayva Liqueur, Leith,
Edinburgh

TYPE Liqueur

STRENGTH 35%

TASTE RATING 2

MINIATURES Yes

COMMENTS Glayva, whose name derives from the Gaelic for 'very good', is a rich, syrupy-textured after-dinner liqueur with a hint of tangerine in its sweet flavours.

BLENDERS Glayva was originally created by Ronald Morrison and Co., an Edinburgh merchants well versed in flavours and bouquets. The combination of aged whisky, syrup of herbs, aromatic oils and honey took many years to perfect. Ownership of Glayva passed to Invergordon when they bought the parent company in 1984.

VISITORS Visitors are accepted by appointment. Telephone 031-554 4404 to arrange.

GLEN ALBYN

Glen Albyn Distillery, Inverness,
Inverness-shire

TYPE Single malt

BOTTLING AGE Varies

STRENGTH Varies

TASTE RATING 3

MINIATURES Yes

COMMENTS This whisky is
available from independent
bottlers only and is difficult
to come by. It is a medium-
bodied, smooth malt with a hint of smokiness in its
bouquet and taste.

DISTILLERY Glen Albyn was established by the provost
of Inverness in 1840, being rebuilt in a new location
near to the Caledonian Canal over 40 years later. It was
bought by Mackinlay and Birnie (who also owned the
neighbouring Glen Mhor Distillery) in 1920 and was
transferred to Scottish Malt Distillers (SMD), a subsidiary of the Distillers Company Ltd, in 1972. Glen
Albyn was one of several SMD distilleries closed down
in 1983 and it was demolished by United Distillers in
1988.

GLENBURGIE

*The Glenburgie-Glenlivet
Distillery, Forres, Moray*

SINGLE HIGHLAND MALT

GLENBURGIE

TRADE MARK OF PROPRIETORS: J & G STODART LTD

SCOTCH WHISKY

40% VOL   AGED 8 YEARS   70cl

PRODUCT OF SCOTLAND

*SPECIALLY SELECTED, PRODUCED AND
BOTTLED BY AND UNDER THE RESPONSIBILITY OF*
GORDON & MACPHAIL
ELGIN, SCOTLAND, BEV.D. BOTTLED

TYPE Single malt

BOTTLING AGE Varies

STRENGTH Varies

TASTE RATING 3

MINIATURES Yes

COMMENTS A light-bodied, delicate single malt whose sweet, slightly floral taste makes it ideal as an aperitif. It is found relatively rarely in this country, as most goes for export.

DISTILLERY A distillery was said to have been established here in 1810, but production ceased and was not revived until the second half of the nineteenth century. It was bought by James & George Stodart Ltd of Dumbarton who themselves were taken over by Hiram Walker in the 1930s. The distillery was extended in 1958 and is now owned by Allied Distillers.

VISITORS The distillery has no reception centre but visitors are welcome by appointment. Telephone 034385-258 to arrange.

GLENCADAM

Glencadam Distillery,
Brechin, Angus

TYPE Single malt

BOTTLING AGE Varies

STRENGTH Varies

TASTE RATING 3–4

MINIATURES Yes

PURE MALT SCOTCH WHISKY
from
GLENCADAM
Distillery

Proprietors: The Glencadam Distillers Co. Ltd.

75 cl   Bottled by Wm. Cadenhead,   46% vol
18 Golden Square, Aberdeen
Scotland

COMMENTS Glencadam, generally available from independent whisky merchants, has a delicate, fruity bouquet and rich, sweetish flavour with a smooth, well-rounded finish.

DISTILLERY Glencadam was built around 1825 and was one of two distilleries in Brechin dating from this decade (North Port being the other). It takes its water from Moorfoot Loch. It is owned by Allied Distillers and is associated with their subsidiary, Stewart & Son of Dundee. Most of its production goes into the blend Stewart's Cream of the Barley.

VISITORS The distillery has no reception centre but visitors are welcome by appointment. Telephone 03562-2217 to arrange.

GLEN CALDER

Gordon and MacPhail, Elgin, Moray

TYPE Blend

STRENGTH 40%

TASTE RATING 2

MINIATURES Yes

COMMENTS A very pleasant blend with a smooth, honey-like nose and light, slightly smoky finish.

PRODUCERS Gordon and MacPhail started in business in 1895 as a licensed grocers and wine and spirit merchant, as had done so many of the foremost names among the Scotch whisky blending industry. Unlike the others, however, Gordon and MacPhail have retained all the original aspects of their business as well as extending into vatting, blending and bottling, and they are today the world's leading malt whisky specialists. Some of the formulas for their blends date from the turn of the century. Glen Calder is one of the most popular blends in northern Scotland and won a Silver Award at the 1981 International Wine and Spirits Competition.

VISITORS Gordon and MacPhail's shop, South St, Elgin is open 0900–1715 Mon.–Wed. (0900–1300 Wed. in winter), 0830–1715 Thu.–Fri., 0900–1700 Sat.

125

GLEN DEVERON

Macduff Distillery, Banff, Banffshire

TYPE Single malt

BOTTLING AGE 12 years

STRENGTH 40%

TASTE RATING 3–4

MINIATURES Yes

COMMENTS A very pleasant Highland malt with a smooth, mellow taste and fresh bouquet.

DISTILLERY A modern distillery, built in 1960, Macduff is one of the few distilleries to give its single malt a different name from its own (although independent bottlers do market the whisky, including miniatures, as 'Macduff'). Water is used for cooling from the nearby River Deveron which gives the malt its name. Macduff Distillery is now owned by William Lawson Distillers, a subsidiary of the General Beveridge Corporation of Luxembourg.

VISITORS Visitors are welcome by appointment. Telephone 0261-2612 to arrange.

GLENDRONACH

The Glendronach Distillery, Forgue,
Huntly, Aberdeenshire

TYPE Single malt

BOTTLING AGE 12 years

STRENGTH 40%, 43%

TASTE RATING 3

MINIATURES Yes

COMMENTS Glendronach is a
beautifully rounded single malt
whose slight peaty tones are balanced by a lingering sweetness.

DISTILLERY The distillery, set picturesquely on the
Dronach Burn in the Aberdeenshire countryside, is one
of the most attractive in the Highlands. Built in 1826,
it was one of the first to be licensed, and its whisky
enjoyed a wide reputation in the nineteenth century. Its
original hand-turned malting floor and coal-fired stills
have been retained. For many years it was operated by
William Teacher & Sons, which became part of Allied
Distillers in 1988.

VISITORS Visitors are welcome by appointment.
Telephone 046682-202 to arrange.

GLENDULLAN

Glendullan Distillery, Dufftown, Keith, Banffshire

TYPE Single malt

BOTTLING AGE 12 years

STRENGTH 43%

TASTE RATING 3

MINIATURES Yes

COMMENTS A good single malt with a robust character yet a mellow, fruity flavour.

DISTILLERY This is one of the seven Dufftown distilleries, built just before the turn of the century and picturesquely set on the banks of the Fiddich. Built for William Williams of Aberdeen, it passed to the control of the newly merged company of Macdonald Greenlees & Williams after the First World War and, with its parent company, into the ownership of the Distillers Company Ltd in 1926. As well as being bottled as a single malt, Glendullan is an important component of Old Parr and of President, a de luxe blend.

VISITORS Visitors are welcome by appointment. Telephone 0340-20250 to arrange.

128

GLENFARCLAS

Glenfarclas Distillery, Marypark,
Ballindalloch, Banffshire

TYPE Single malt

BOTTLING AGE 10, 12, 15, 21,
25 years

STRENGTH 40%, 43%, 46%,
60%

TASTE RATING 3-4, 5 (60%)

MINIATURES Yes

COMMENTS Glenfarclas is a
whisky of true character, and is
widely acknowledged as one of
the classic malts. It has a rich,
sherry bouquet, a well-rounded,
fruity body and a delicious, mellow finish.

DISTILLERY Glenfarclas is one
of the few independently owned
distilleries left in the Highlands.
Founded in 1836, it was bought
by J & G Grant in 1865 and is
still in family hands. It is set in an isolated spot by Ben
Rinnes yet attracts in excess of 60,000 visitors a year to
its well-maintained visitor facilities.

GLENFARCLAS cont.

VISITORS The distillery is on the Whisky Trail and visitors are welcome 0900–1630 Mon.–Fri., 1000–1600 Sat., June–Sept.; 1000–1600 Mon.–Fri., Oct.–May; or by appointment. Large parties should telephone in advance. Telephone 08072-245.

GLENFIDDICH

Glenfiddich Distillery, Dufftown,
Keith, Banffshire

TYPE Single malt

BOTTLING AGE No age given

STRENGTH 40%

TASTE RATING 2

MINIATURES Yes

COMMENTS Possibly the world's best-known malt, Glenfiddich has a light, peaty aroma with a smooth, counterbalancing sweetness. An excellent introduction to malt whisky, and ideal, too, as an aperitif.

DISTILLERY Glenfiddich Distillery was started by William Grant, a former apprentice shoemaker who worked at Mortlach, another Dufftown distillery, until he gained enough knowledge and money to set up on his own in 1887. The new distillery was successful as soon as it went into production, and has remained so ever since, thanks not only to the quality and accessibility of its product but also to far-sighted marketing. The distillery is part of the largest family-owned independent whisky company.

VISITORS The distillery is on the Whisky Trail and visitors are welcome 0930–1630 Mon.–Fri. all year; 0930–1630 Sat., 1200–1630 Sun., Easter–mid Oct. Large parties should telephone in advance. Telephone 0340-20373.

GLEN GARIOCH

Glengarioch Distillery, Oldmeldrum,
Aberdeenshire

TYPE Single malt

BOTTLING AGE 8, 10, 12, 15, 21 years

STRENGTH 43%

TASTE RATING 3

MINIATURES Yes

COMMENTS This medium-bodied whisky, with its light texture and smoky flavour, is an ideal after-dinner dram.

DISTILLERY Set in the Aberdeenshire market town of Oldmeldrum, Glengarioch was reputedly founded in the 1790s. It has had several owners, and was sold by the Distillers Company Ltd in 1970 to Morrison, two years after its closure because of a shortage of water. Morrison have not only sunk a deep well but have introduced other improvements, including the recycling of heated water to warm tomatoes and other glasshouse plants.

VISITORS Visitors are welcome by appointment. Telephone 06512-2706 to arrange.

133

GLENGLASSAUGH

Glenglassaugh Distillery,
Portsoy, Banffshire

TYPE Single malt

BOTTLING AGE No age
given

STRENGTH 40%

TASTE RATING 3

MINIATURES Yes

COMMENTS A smooth single
malt of light-to-medium
body with a certain richness in its tones.

DISTILLERY Built in 1875, the distillery takes its water
supplies from springs in the nearby hills. It was bought
by Highland Distilleries in 1892, and almost completely
rebuilt in the late 1950s, making it one of the most
modern distilleries in the Highlands, although it has
since been mothballed.

GLENGOYNE

Glengoyne Distillery, Dumgoyne,
Stirlingshire

TYPE Single malt

BOTTLING AGE 10, 12, 17 years

STRENGTH 40%, 43%

TASTE RATING 2–3

MINIATURES Yes

COMMENTS A light, pleasant, sweetish whisky with a fragrant aroma and no abrasive edges. Ideal as an aperitif.

DISTILLERY Glengoyne stands just north of the Highland Line (the line initiated by the Customs and Excise to differentiate area boundaries between styles of whisky) and so qualifies as a Highland distillery. It was built in 1833 (when it was known as Burnfoot) at the foot of the Campsie Fells, near the 50-foot waterfall from which it takes its supplies. It was bought by Lang Brothers in 1876 and was sympathetically restored and extended in the 1960s.

VISITORS Visitors are welcome during working hours, Mon.–Sat. Large parties (of ten and over) are requested to make prior bookings. Telephone 041-332 6361 to arrange.

GLEN GRANT

Glen Grant Distillery, Rothes, Moray

TYPE Single malt

BOTTLING AGE 5, 10 years

STRENGTH 40%, 43%

TASTE RATING 2

MINIATURES Yes

COMMENTS A highly regarded
Speyside single malt. The five years
old is light and dry, making it ideal as
an aperitif, while the older version has a
sweeter, fruitier, more rounded character.

DISTILLERY Opened by James and John Grant in 1840,
Glen Grant enjoyed continuous expansion throughout
the last century, and this has continued to the present day.
The company was amalgamated with the Smiths of
Glenlivet in the 1950s to form The Glenlivet and Glen
Grant Distillers, which in turn merged with the
Edinburgh blending firm of Hill Thomson in 1970 to
form The Glenlivet Distillers. Glen Grant is now part of
Seagram.

VISITORS The distillery is on the Whisky Trail and
visitors are welcome 1000–1600 Mon.–Fri., Easter–
end Sept. Telephone 03403-413.

GLEN KEITH

Glen Keith Distillery,
Keith, Banffshire

CONNOISSEURS CHOICE

Connoisseurs Choice, a range of single malts from various districts of Scotland

In the Highlands are situated the greatest number of malt whisky distilleries

SINGLE HIGHLAND
MALT SCOTCH WHISKY
DISTILLED AT
GLEN KEITH
DISTILLERY
Proprietors: Chivas Bros. Ltd

DISTILLED 1965 DISTILLED

70cl SPECIALLY SELECTED, PRODUCED AND BOTTLED BY
GORDON & MACPHAIL
ELGIN · SCOTLAND
PRODUCT OF SCOTLAND 40%vol

TYPE Single malt

BOTTLING AGE Varies

STRENGTH Varies

TASTE RATING 2

MINIATURES Yes

COMMENTS A difficult-to-find, smooth and sweet-tasting Speyside single malt which is occasionally available from independent bottlers.

DISTILLERY Glen Keith was built by Chivas Brothers in 1958, across the River Isla from Strathisla, another of their distilleries and one of the oldest in Scotland. As if by deliberate contrast, processes used at Glen Keith are innovative, and it was the first of the Scotch whisky distilleries to have its production processes automated.

VISITORS The distillery is not open to visitors.

GLENKINCHIE

Glenkinchie Distillery, Pencaitland, Trenant, East Lothian

TYPE Single malt

BOTTLING AGE 10 years

STRENGTH 43%

TASTE RATING 3

MINIATURES Yes

COMMENTS Ideal as an aperitif, Glenkinchie is the driest and smokiest of Lowland whiskies. It is a fine, pale, smooth malt.

DISTILLERY Glenkinchie takes its name from the burn which flows by it and the glen in which it stands. It was established in the late 1830s and has been in production since, except during the wars. The licence is held by Haig, the brand owned by United Distillers, and most of Glenkinchie's product goes into their blends.

VISITORS Visitors are welcome 0930–1630 Mon.–Fri. Telephone 0875-340451.

THE GLENLIVET

The Glenlivet Distillery, Ballindalloch, Banffshire

TYPE Single malt

BOTTLING AGE 12, 21 years

STRENGTH 40%, 43%

TASTE RATING 3–4

MINIATURES Yes

COMMENTS The Glenlivet is a subtly balanced malt. Its light, delicate bouquet has traces of fruit, and floral notes, while the complex flavours are delicately balanced between a medium sweetness and smooth dryness.

DISTILLERY This was one of the first distilleries licensed under the reforming 1823 Licensing Act – a fact which so incensed his still-illegal neighbours that its founder, George Smith, was obliged to carry pistols for his own protection. The whisky so grew in popularity that other distillers adopted the name, and an ensuing legal case and settlement (which endures to this day) allowed the Smiths to use the direct article in their whisky's name while others were to use it as a hyphenated suffix. The Glenlivet is still one of the most popular whiskies worldwide.

VISITORS The distillery is on the Whisky Trail and visitors are welcome 1000–1700 Mon.–Sat.; and 1000–1900 Mon.–Sat., July–Aug. Telephone 08073-427.

GLENLOCHY

Glenlochy Distillery, Fort William, Inverness-shire

TYPE Single malt

BOTTLING AGE Varies

STRENGTH Varies

TASTE RATING 2

MINIATURES Yes

COMMENTS A floral bouquet leads into a clean, dryish-tasting malt with a rather quick finish. Light-bodied and good as an aperitif.

CONNOISSEURS CHOICE

Connoisseurs Choice: a range of single malts from various distilleries of Scotland

In the Highlands are situated the greatest number of malt whisky distilleries.

SINGLE HIGHLAND
MALT SCOTCH WHISKY
DISTILLED AT

GLENLOCHY
DISTILLERY
PROPRIETORS: D. & J. McCallum Ltd

DISTILLED 1974 DISTILLED

SPECIALLY SELECTED PRODUCED AND BOTTLED BY

GORDON & MACPHAIL

ELGIN · SCOTLAND
PRODUCT OF SCOTLAND

75cl   40%vol

DISTILLERY Glenlochy Distillery was built close to Loch Lochy at the southern end of the Caledonian Canal in a pretty setting on the outskirts of Fort William. It was built in 1900 with production beginning the following year. The single malt product is now something of a rarity, as the distillery was closed by its parent company, United Distillers, in the 1980s, and sold outside the industry in 1991.

GLENLOSSIE

*Glenlossie-Glenlivet Distillery,
Birnie, Elgin, Moray*

TYPE Single malt

BOTTLING AGE 10 years

STRENGTH 43%

TASTE RATING 2

MINIATURES Yes

COMMENTS Another
whisky which is difficult to find, Glenlossie has a fresh,
grassy aroma with a touch of fruitiness and a smooth,
lingering flavour.

DISTILLERY Glenlossie was built not far from the River
Lossie in 1876 by a former distillery manager-turned-
hotel owner from Lhanbryde, near Elgin. It was expanded and improved between 1896 and 1917. In 1962, its
stills were increased from four to six, while in 1992 a new
mash tun was fitted. The licensee is presently Haig and
the distillery is owned by United Distillers.

VISITORS Visitors are welcome by appointment.
Telephone 0343-86331 to arrange.

GLEN MHOR

Glen Mhor Distillery, Inverness, Inverness-shire

TYPE Single malt

BOTTLING AGE Varies

STRENGTH Varies

TASTE RATING 3

MINIATURES Yes

COMMENTS Smooth and medium-bodied, Glen Mhor has a pleasant, subtle sweetness complemented by a dryish, heathery aftertaste.

DISTILLERY This distillery was built between 1892 and 1894 by Mackinlay and Birnie who were later to own the neighbouring Glen Albyn Distillery; John Birnie had previously managed Glen Albyn. Glen Mhor used the same water (from Loch Ness) and peat as its neighbour, but their whiskies were quite different. It was one of the first distilleries in Scotland to introduce mechanical malting in the late 1940s. It was also one of the Scottish Malt Distillers distilleries closed down by the Distillers Company Ltd in 1983 and was demolished in 1988.

GLENMORANGIE

Glenmorangie Distillery, Tain, Ross-shire

TYPE Single malt

BOTTLING AGE 10, 18 years

STRENGTH 40%, 43%

TASTE RATING 3–4

MINIATURES Yes

COMMENTS A smooth and medium bodied whisky, with a delicate, slightly sweet aroma. Scotland's best-selling single malt.

DISTILLERY Distilling was begun here in 1843 by the Mathieson family as a sideline to farming. In 1918, The Glenmorangie Distillery Company passed into the control of its present owners, Macdonald and Muir Ltd, later to become part of Macdonald Martin. Water is supplied by unusually hard, mineral-rich springs in the nearby Tarlogie Forest, peat is brought in from Aberdeenshire, and charred American oak barrels are used in

the maturation process. The distillery is unusual in that
all its output goes into its single malt.

VISITORS Visitors are welcome by appointment.
Telephone 086289-2043 to arrange.

GLEN MORAY

Glen Moray-Glenlivet Distillery,
Elgin, Moray

TYPE Single malt

BOTTLING AGE 12 years,
various vintages (1960–67)

STRENGTH 40%, 43%

TASTE RATING 2–3

MINIATURES Yes

COMMENTS Golden in
colour, with a soft, fresh
bouquet leading into a smooth and rounded taste. Ideal
for drinking at any time, it is the sister malt to the
better-known Glenmorangie.

DISTILLERY Established during the whisky boom years
of the 1890s, the Glen Moray-Glenlivet Distillery was
expanded in 1958. It is controlled by Macdonald
Martin, and in addition to its availability as a single
malt, its produce also features in many well-known
blends.

VISITORS Visitors are welcome by appointment.
Telephone 0343-542577 to arrange.

GLEN ORD

Glen Ord Distillery,
Muir of Ord, Ross-shire

TYPE Single malt

BOTTLING AGE 12 years

STRENGTH 40%

TASTE RATING 2–3

MINIATURES Yes

COMMENTS A smooth, well-rounded, slightly dry malt with a fragrant bouquet and mellow finish.

DISTILLERY This distillery stands in an area which was infamous for illicit distillation even as late as a century ago. It stands on a tributary of the River Conan, the Oran Burn, whose clear waters have been used by legal and illegal whisky producers alike. Ord Distillery, as it then was, was founded in 1838 on land leased from the Mackenzies of Ord to provide a ready market for barley produced on Mackenzie farms. It was acquired by Dewar's in 1923, and is now owned by United Distillers.

VISITORS Visitors are welcome 0930–1700 Mon.–Fri. Telephone 0463-870421.

THE GLEN ROTHES

Glen Rothes Distillery, Rothes, Moray

TYPE Single malt

BOTTLING AGE 12 years

STRENGTH 43%

TASTE RATING 3–4

MINIATURES Yes

COMMENTS A popular, full-bodied single malt with distinctively peaty characteristics and a pleasing dryness to its aftertaste.

DISTILLERY The Glen Rothes Distillery was built in 1878 for William Grant & Sons with the backing of a group of local businessmen, including the provost of Rothes. It was bought in 1887 by the Islay Distillery Company, owners of Bunnahabhain, and became part of the Highland Distilleries company. The distillery has been expanded twice in the last 30 years. The Glen Rothes is distributed worldwide by Berry Brothers and Rudd, the owners of Cutty Sark whisky.

VISITORS Visitors are welcome by appointment. Telephone 041-332 7511 to arrange.

GLEN SCOTIA

Glen Scotia Distillery,
Campbeltown, Argyllshire

TYPE Single malt

BOTTLING AGE 12 years

STRENGTH 40%

TASTE RATING 3

MINIATURES Yes

COMMENTS Glen Scotia is a rich, peaty, oily malt with
a pungent aroma and a smooth, well-rounded finish.

DISTILLERY Scotia, as it was previously known, was one
of 32 Campbeltown distilleries operating last century,
partly explaining why the town has its own regional
classification, even though only two distilleries remain.
Glen Scotia Distillery was built in 1835 and has had
many owners, the ghost of one of whom is said to haunt
the place.

VISITORS The distillery is not open to visitors.

GLENTAUCHERS

Glentauchers Distillery,
Mulben, Banffshire

TYPE Single malt

BOTTLING AGE Varies

STRENGTH Varies

TASTE RATING 2

MINIATURES Yes

COMMENTS The sweetness of Glentauchers' aroma and taste are balanced by the light dryness of its finish. A nice pre-dinner dram, but generally available only from independent merchants.

DISTILLERY Glentauchers was built in 1898 by James Buchanan, the entrepreneur responsible for the success of Black & White whisky. The distillery was largely rebuilt and modernized in 1965. It was silent for a number of years in the 1980s until Allied Distillers acquired it from United Distillers in 1988 and immediately reopened it.

VISITORS The distillery has no reception centre but visitors are welcome by appointment. Telephone 05426-272 to arrange.

THE GLENTURRET

Glenturret Distillery, The Hosh,
Crieff, Perthshire

TYPE Single malt

BOTTLING AGE 8, 12, 15, 21,
25 years

STRENGTH 40%

TASTE RATING 3–4

MINIATURES Yes

COMMENTS Glenturret is an award-winning, full-bodied
Highland malt with a rich, nutty flavour and nicely
rounded finish.

DISTILLERY Glenturret stands in a lovely position on
the banks of the River Turret, in an area where smuggling
and illicit distillation were rife in the past. It is probable
that the distillery's own eighteenth-century origins lie
there. Glenturret was closed from the 1920s until 1959,
when it was largely rebuilt. Facilities for visitors are
among the best of any distillery.

VISITORS Visitors are welcome by appointment.
Telephone 0764-2424 to arrange.

GLENUGIE

Glenugie Distillery, Peterhead,
Aberdeenshire

TYPE Single malt

BOTTLING AGE Varies

STRENGTH Varies

TASTE RATING 2

MINIATURES Yes

COMMENTS A medium-bodied whisky with a sweetish, malty flavour and a fruity aroma. Available from independent bottlers.

DISTILLERY Glenugie was the easternmost distillery in Scotland, located in the harbour town of Peterhead. The distillery was first established in the 1830s, and was completely rebuilt in 1875. It was closed in 1982 and although there were never any bottlings under the distillery's own label, supplies from the independent merchants are still available.

HAIG

United Distillers, Banbeath, Leven, Fife

TYPE Blend

STRENGTH 40%

TASTE RATING 2

MINIATURES Yes

COMMENTS A nicely balanced whisky with a fragrant aroma, Haig is smooth and easy to drink, with a long, sweet finish.

BLENDERS Haig is a family name long associated with the whisky industry, going back almost 350 years, when Robert Haig, a farmer of Stirlingshire, was rebuked by his local church for distilling his whisky on a Sunday. The family had connections by marriage to the Steins, another of the big Lowland distilling families, and the Jamesons, the Dublin whiskey distillers. The Haigs were instrumental in introducing new practices and machinery (for example, the new patent still in the 1830s) to the grain distilleries which they built in Edinburgh and the east. The company was acquired by the Distillers Company in 1919. As well as the de luxe Dimple, the company also produces Glenleven, a 12-year-old vatted malt with a malty aroma and a hint of peat in its taste.

HEATHER CREAM

Inver House Distillers, Moffat Distillery, Airdrie, Lanarkshire

TYPE Cream Liqueur

STRENGTH 17%

TASTE RATING 2

MINIATURES Yes

COMMENTS Heather Cream is a sweet blend of cream and malt whisky, and is one of the most popular of the Scotch whisky cream liqueurs available today.

BLENDERS Heather Cream's producers, Inver House, also own Knockdhu (producing An Cnoc) and Speyburn-Glenlivet distilleries, and produce Pinwinnie de luxe blend, among others. Heather Cream is produced at their complex at Moffat Distillery on the outskirts of Airdrie; a converted former paper mill, it also holds a grain distillery.

VISITORS The distillery and plant are not open to visitors.

HIGHLAND PARK

Highland Park Distillery, Kirkwall, Orkney

TYPE Single malt

BOTTLING AGE 12 years

STRENGTH 40%

TASTE RATING 3–4

MINIATURES Yes

COMMENTS The different nature of Orcadian peat is said to be a factor in the quite distinctive qualities of the islands' whiskies. Highland Park is a medium-bodied single malt of character, with a heathery–smoky aroma and peaty flavour with balancing sweet tones.

DISTILLERY Highland Park's origins are linked with an illegal bothy which previously occupied the site. Its owner was one of whisky's most colourful characters, Magnus Eunson. A United Presbyterian church elder by day and smuggler by night, he was not averse to hiding his whisky below the church pulpit, among other places. The legal distillery was founded in 1798 and passed to the Grant family in 1895. Highland Distilleries purchased it in 1937.

VISITORS Visitors are welcome 1000–1600 Mon.–Fri., Easter–end Sept., and other times by appointment. Large groups should telephone in advance. Telephone 0856-874619 to arrange.

IMMORTAL MEMORY

Gordon and MacPhail, Elgin, Moray

TYPE Blend

BOTTLING AGE 8 years

STRENGTH 40%

TASTE RATING 2

MINIATURES Yes

COMMENTS A blend which is floral on the nose — perhaps with a hint of parma violets — with a nutty flavour and a warming finish.

PRODUCERS Gordon and MacPhail started in business in 1895 as a licensed grocers and wine and spirit merchant, as had done so many of the foremost names among the Scotch whisky blending industry. Unlike the others, however, Gordon and MacPhail have retained all the original aspects of their business as well as extending into vatting, blending and bottling. This blend was declared 'Best Blended Whisky in the World' at the 1991 International Wine and Spirit Competition.

VISITORS Gordon and MacPhail's shop, South St, Elgin is open 0900–1715 Mon.–Wed. (0900–1300 Wed. in winter), 0830–1715 Thu.–Fri., 0900–1700 Sat.

IMPERIAL

Imperial Distillery, Carron, Moray

TYPE Single malt

BOTTLING AGE Varies

STRENGTH Varies

TASTE RATING 4

MINIATURES Yes

COMMENTS A full-bodied malt with bags of character, Imperial contrives to balance a rich sweetness with a lingering smokiness. Available from independent merchants.

DISTILLERY Imperial was established in 1897, the year of Queen Victoria's Diamond Jubilee, by Thomas Mackenzie, who already owned Dailuaine and Talisker. All three distilleries were combined under the name of Dailuaine-Talisker Distilleries Ltd. Imperial Distillery was modernized in the mid 1950s. Production was halted temporarily in the 1980s, but was restarted again after Imperial's purchase by Allied Distillers in 1988.

VISITORS The distillery has no reception centre but visitors are welcome by appointment. Telephone 03406-276 to arrange.

40% vol.   *Product of Scotland*   70 cl.

IMPERIAL

TRADE MARK OF PROPRIETORS ALLIED DISTILLERS LTD

Single Highland Malt

Scotch **DISTILLED 1979** *Whisky*

IMPERIAL

Built in 1897, the year of
Queen Victoria's Diamond
Jubilee, the Imperial
Distillery stands
majestically among the
dark woods of Carron,
in a fold of the hills
which encompass the
glittering Spey.

Specially selected
produced and bottled by
and under the
responsibility of
Gordon & Macphail,
Elgin, Scotland.
Regd. Bottlers

PURE MALT SCOTCH WHISKY
from

IMPERIAL
Distillery

Proprietors: Dailuaine-Talisker Distilleries Ltd.

75 cl   Bottled by Wm. Cadenhead,
18 Golden Square, Aberdeen   46% vol
Scotland

INCHGOWER

Inchgower Distillery, Buckie, Banffshire

TYPE Single malt

BOTTLING AGE 14 years

STRENGTH 43%

TASTE RATING 2–3

MINIATURES Yes

COMMENTS A robust, distinctly heavy-bodied malt with a combination of nutty, fruity and spicy aromas, and a hint of sweetness in its tones.

DISTILLERY Inchgower was moved from Tochineal by its founder, Alexander Wilson, to its present site at Rathaven, near Buckie, to take advantage of the ready supply of water from the Letter Burn and the Springs of Aultmoor. When the original firm went out of business, the distillery passed to Buckie Town Council who sold it to Arthur Bell and Sons for £1000 in 1938. Most of the whisky goes into Bell's blends and the distillery is now owned by United Distillers.

VISITORS Visitors are welcome by appointment. Telephone 0542-31161.

SPEYSIDE
SINGLE MALT
SCOTCH WHISKY

The *Oyster Catcher* is a common sight around the

INCHGOWER

distillery, which stands close to the sea on the mouth of the *RIVER SPEY* near *BUCKIE*. Inchgower, established in 1824, produces one of the most distinctive single malt whiskies in *SPEYSIDE*. It is a must for the discerning drinker ~ a complex aroma precedes a fruity, spicy taste ⚜ with a hint of salt.

AGED **14** YEARS

INCHMURRIN

*Loch Lomond Distillery, Alexandria,
Dunbartonshire*

TYPE Single malt

BOTTLING AGE No age given

STRENGTH 40%

TASTE RATING 2

MINIATURES Yes

COMMENTS A clean, light, pre-
dinner malt with a fresh, floral
note. A Highland malt with a
Lowland character.

DISTILLERY A relatively recent addition to the ranks of
Scotland's distilleries, Loch Lomond was founded in
1966 on the site of an old printing and bleaching plant.
Like Glengoyne, it just qualifies as being a Highland
malt and is situated just to the south of the famous loch.

VISITORS The distillery is not open to visitors.

INVERGORDON

Invergordon Distillery,
Invergordon, Ross-shire

TYPE Grain

BOTTLING AGE 10 years

STRENGTH 43%

TASTE RATING 2

MINIATURES Yes

COMMENTS A light, clean, smooth whisky with a gentle and slightly vanilla-like taste.

DISTILLERY Built in the late 1950s to provide work in an area of high unemployment, Invergordon grain distillery is now one of the biggest distilleries in Europe. Like other distilleries in the area, a provost of Inverness had a hand in its establishment. Ben Wyvis malt distillery was added on the same site but is now closed. With four other distilleries with which to reciprocate, Invergordon is in an excellent position to control and produce its own blends.

VISITORS The distillery is not open to visitors.

INVERLEVEN

Inverleven Distillery, Dumbarton, Dunbartonshire

TYPE Single malt

BOTTLING AGE Varies

STRENGTH Varies

TASTE RATING 2

MINIATURES Yes

COMMENTS A relatively smooth Lowland malt, with a nice balance of dry and sweet flavours. Available from independent whisky merchants only.

DISTILLERY Built in 1938, Inverleven is part of a modern-looking red-brick plant, which includes Dumbarton grain distillery, on the banks of the Leven in Dumbarton. It stands on the Highland Line (the line initiated by the Customs and Excise to differentiate area boundaries between styles of whisky), and is counted as a Lowland distillery. It is owned by Allied Distillers and almost all of its output goes into their blends, which include Ballantine's, Teacher's, Long John and Black Bottle.

VISITORS The distillery is not suitable for visitors.

ISLAY MIST

MacDuff International, Glasgow

TYPE De luxe

BOTTLING AGE Varies

STRENGTH 40%

TASTE RATING 3

MINIATURES No

COMMENTS This de luxe blend instantly betrays its origins, though as the name suggests, it is mellower in taste than its main component, Laphroaig. Islay Mist is matured in oak casks and is ideal as an introduction for those wishing to sample the delights of the Islay whiskies. A 17-year-old version is also available.

BLENDERS The blenders of Islay Mist, MacDuff International, are a new, independent Scotch whisky company, established in 1992. As well as Islay Mist, their product range includes Lauder's, one of the oldest blends in the Scotch whisky market, Grand MacNish and Strathbeag blends.

VISITORS The blending and bottling plant is not open to visitors.

ISLE OF JURA

Isle of Jura Distillery, Craighouse,
Jura, Argyllshire

TYPE Single malt

BOTTLING AGE 10 years

STRENGTH 40%, 43%

TASTE RATING 3

MINIATURES Yes

COMMENTS Reminiscent of a Highland malt, though with a light, clean, fragrant palate of its own, this Island malt is ideal as an aperitif.

DISTILLERY The distillery is one of the main employers on this island of around 200 inhabitants. It was first built overlooking the Sound of Jura in 1810, next to a cave where illicit distillation may have been carried on for as long as three centuries. The distillery's machinery and buildings were owned by different individuals, and a dispute between the two led to its closure for over 50 years in 1913. It was effectively redesigned and rebuilt before its reopening in the 1960s.

VISITORS Visitors are welcome by appointment. Telephone 049682-240 to arrange.

163

J & B RARE

Justerini and Brooks, London

TYPE Blend

STRENGTH 40%, 43%

TASTE RATING 2

MINIATURES Yes

COMMENTS J & B Rare is a smooth, sweet-tasting whisky with a light, fresh character. It is the second-best selling Scotch whisky in the world.

BLENDERS Justerini and Brooks' principal founder, Giacomo Justerini, was a distiller from Bologna who was infatuated by an Italian opera singer, whom he followed to London in the mid-eighteenth century. In London, he found a partner to finance the production of his liqueurs; after his partner's death his share was bought by the eponymous Brooks in 1831. In 1962 the company amalgamated with four others to form International Distillers and Vintners Ltd (IDV), taking control of the running of Knockando, Glen Spey and Strathmill distilleries. A new distillery, Auchroisk, was built by IDV in 1974. Grand Metropolitan bought IDV, then part of Watney Mann & Truman, in 1972. As well as the popular J & B Rare, the company also produces J & B Reserve, a more mature 15-year-old blend.

BY APPOINTMENT TO HER MAJESTY THE QUEEN
WINE MERCHANTS
JUSTERINI & BROOKS LTD.
19 ST. JAMES'S STREET, LONDON, ENGLAND

RARE
A BLEND OF THE PUREST
OLD SCOTCH WHISKIES

DISTILLED, BLENDED AND BOTTLED IN SCOTLAND

JUSTERINI & BROOKS LTD.
St. James's Street, London, England

BY APPOINTMENT TO THEIR LATE MAJESTIES
KING GEORGE III

KING GEORGE IV	KING EDWARD VII
KING WILLIAM IV	KING GEORGE V
QUEEN VICTORIA	KING GEORGE VI

AND TO HIS LATE ROYAL HIGHNESS
THE PRINCE OF WALES (1921-1936)

AND TO H.R.H. THE PRINCE OF THE NETHERLANDS

PRODUCT OF SCOTLAND

75cl   43% vol.

75cl   43% vol.

BY APPOINTMENT TO HER MAJESTY THE QUEEN
WINE MERCHANTS JUSTERINI & BROOKS LTD.
19 ST. JAMES'S STREET, LONDON, ENGLAND

RESERVE
15 YEARS OLD

A BLEND OF THE PUREST
OLD SCOTCH WHISKIES

DISTILLED, BLENDED AND BOTTLED IN SCOTLAND BY

JUSTERINI & BROOKS LTD.
St. James's Street, London, England
ESTABLISHED 1749

PRODUCT OF SCOTLAND

JOHNNIE WALKER BLACK LABEL

United Distillers, Kilmarnock, Ayrshire

TYPE De luxe

BOTTLING AGE 12 years

STRENGTH 40%

TASTE RATING 2–3

MINIATURES Yes

COMMENTS One of the most successful de luxe whiskies, with a special quality of smoothness and a depth of taste and character which linger on the palate.

BLENDERS In common with other entrepreneurs who became the major operators in the whisky-blending industry, the original Johnnie Walker began as a licensed grocer in Kilmarnock in 1820. It was his grandsons who created the Black Label and Red Label blends in the early 1900s. His son, Alexander Walker, bought Cardow Distillery in 1893, thus ensuring a regular supply of malt for their blends. In 1925 the company joined the Distillers Company Ltd who bought the Talisker and Dailuaine distilleries and licensed the former to Walker. It is probable that malt from it, and from Cardhu, is used in the production of both Walker blends.

JOHNNIE WALKER BLUE LABEL

United Distillers,
Kilmarnock, Ayrshire

TYPE **Blend**

STRENGTH **40%**

TASTE RATING **2–3**

MINIATURES **No**

COMMENTS Blue Label is among the most exclusive of blended whiskies, with a subtle and complex character and a rich, pleasing flavour.

BLENDERS Introduced to the UK market in October 1992 under its new name, Blue Label is the latest addition to the family of Johnnie Walker whiskies. Previously known as Johnnie Walker Oldest, it is among the most expensive of all blended whiskies available in the UK today. Most of the product is intended to go for export, particularly to Japanese markets. The Johnnie Walker company was begun as a licensed grocer in the early nineteenth century and is now one of the major blending names under the United Distillers flag.

JOHNNIE WALKER RED LABEL

United Distillers,
Kilmarnock, Ayrshire

TYPE Blend

STRENGTH 40%

TASTE RATING 2

MINIATURES Yes

COMMENTS A smooth blend with sweet and dry notes of maltiness and peatiness. Red Label is the world's biggest-selling blended whisky.

BLENDERS In common with other entrepreneurs who became the major operators in the whisky-blending industry, the original Johnnie Walker began as a licensed grocer in Kilmarnock in 1820. It was his grandsons who created the Black Label and Red Label blends in the early 1900s. His son, Alexander Walker, bought Cardow Distillery in 1893, thus ensuring a regular supply of malt for their blends. In 1925 the company joined the Distillers Company Ltd who bought the Talisker and Dailuaine distilleries and licensed the former to Walker. It is probable that malt from it, and from Cardhu, is used in the production of both Walker blends.

KNOCKANDO

Knockando Distillery, Knockando,
Aberlour, Banffshire

TYPE Single malt

BOTTLING AGE Bottled when ready,
rather than pre-determined age;
always at least 12 years

STRENGTH 40%, 43%

TASTE RATING 3–4

MINIATURES Yes

COMMENTS Knockando is a light, easy-to-drink single
malt, with pleasantly smooth, nutty hints.

DISTILLERY Built during the 1890s whisky boom,
Knockando is today owned by International Distillers and
Vintners. The distillery's name is said to mean 'small black
hill', and Knockando itself is set on a hill overlooking the
Spey. Knockando single malt is bottled only when it is
considered to have reached its peak rather than at a pre-
determined age – generally, this is between twelve and
fifteen years. The label lists the year of distillation – the
'season' – and the year of bottling. Such season dating
recalls the time when Scottish distilleries only distilled
during the winter season after the barley harvest.

VISITORS Visitors are welcome by appointment.
Telephone 0340-6205 to arrange.

LAGAVULIN

Lagavulin Distillery, Port Ellen,
Islay, Argyllshire

TYPE Single malt

BOTTLING AGE 16 years

STRENGTH 43%

TASTE RATING 5

MINIATURES Yes

COMMENTS A distinctively Islay malt, powerful and demanding, with a dominant aroma and a dry, peaty–smoky flavour complemented by a trace of sweetness.

DISTILLERY Distilling was carried on in this area from the 1740s, when moonshiners made and smuggled illicit whisky to the mainland. Lagavulin's own history is entangled with these times, although the distillery dates officially from the 1810s. Lagavulin's owners went into partnership with the Mackie company, who subsequently became the White Horse Company, and the whisky is still used in White Horse blends today. The distillery is presently owned by United Distillers.

VISITORS Visitors are welcome by appointment. Telephone 0496-2400/2250 to arrange.

LAPHROAIG

*Laphroaig Distillery, Port Ellen,
Islay, Argyllshire*

TYPE Single malt

BOTTLING AGE 10, 15 years

STRENGTH 40%, 43%, up
to 45.1%

TASTE RATING 5

MINIATURES Yes

COMMENTS A robust, full-bodied, classic Islay malt with
a trace of seaweed in its strongly peaty flavour.

DISTILLERY Laphroaig Distillery is set on a bay on
Islay's southern shore, and dates back to 1815. It is a traditional distillery and one of the few still to have a
hand-turned malting floor, ensuring the traditional taste.
It is controlled by Allied Distillers, and Laphroaig is
one of the components in their Long John, Black Bottle,
Ballantine's and Teacher's blends.

VISITORS Visitors are welcome by appointment,
Sept.—end June. Telephone 0496-2418 to arrange.

LEDAIG

Tobermory Distillery, Tobermory, Mull, Argyllshire

LEDAIG
SINGLE MALT
FROM
THE ISLE OF MULL

1974
Vintage

BOTTLED 1992

This rare old single whisky
was distilled at the Ledaig Distillery
on the Isle of Mull by
Ledaig Distillers (Tobermory) Ltd.

PRODUCE OF SCOTLAND

TYPE Single malt

BOTTLING AGE 18, 19, 20 years

STRENGTH 40%

TASTE RATING 5

MINIATURES Yes

COMMENTS A full-bodied single malt from the Tobermory Distillery, Ledaig has strongly peaty flavours.

DISTILLERY Set in a wooded site by the sea, Tobermory Distillery has enjoyed mixed fortunes since it was first established in 1823. It has been closed several times during its existence, most recently in the 1980s when it was mothballed. Having reopened in 1990, the distillery is now back in production. The distillery was previously known as Ledaig, changing its name in the 1970s. It is one of the few family-owned independent distilleries.

VISITORS The Visitor Centre and Distillery Shop are open Mon.–Fri. Easter–30 Sept. Tours can be arranged at other times in the year. Telephone 0688-2119.

LINKWOOD

Linkwood Distillery, Elgin, Moray

TYPE Single malt

BOTTLING AGE 12 years

STRENGTH 43%

TASTE RATING 4–5

MINIATURES Yes

COMMENTS Linkwood is widely acclaimed as one of the best Speyside malts, having the area's characteristics in a fine balance: smoky, and with a fruity sweetness underlying its malty tones.

DISTILLERY This is one of the most traditional of distilleries despite extensive rebuilding work carried out three times since its establishment in the 1820s: it is said that equipment was never replaced until absolutely necessary, and even a spider's web was not removed in case the change of environment would affect the whisky. Built by a former provost of Elgin, Linkwood has an attractive wooded setting by Linkwood Burn outside the town. The distillery is now owned by United Distillers.

VISITORS Visitors are welcome by appointment, 0800–1630. Telephone 0343-547004 to arrange.

LITTLEMILL

Littlemill Distillery, Bowling,
Dunbartonshire

TYPE Single malt

BOTTLING AGE 8 years

STRENGTH 43%

TASTE RATING 3

MINIATURES Yes

COMMENTS A light
Lowland malt with a
smooth, sweet flavour. Good as an aperitif.

DISTILLERY Littlemill began life as a brewery centuries
before distilling was started, with its ale apparently cross-
ing the Clyde to supply the monks of Paisley Abbey. It
was established as a distillery in the late eighteenth century and is one of the oldest in Scotland. Its water comes
from the Kilpatrick Hills, to the north of the Highland
Line (the line initiated by the Customs and Excise to differentiate area boundaries between styles of whisky),
although Littlemill is a Lowland distillery and whisky.

VISITORS The distillery is not open to the public.

174

LOCHSIDE

Lochside Distillery,
Montrose, Angus

TYPE Single malt

BOTTLING AGE 10 years

STRENGTH 40%

TASTE RATING 2

MINIATURES No

COMMENTS A light-to-medium bodied single malt with a sweet, fruity aroma and drier, smooth flavour. It is difficult to find under the distillery label, but supplies are also available from independent merchants.

DISTILLERY Established as recently as 1957, Lochside was built on the site of an eighteenth-century brewery. It originally comprised two distilleries, one grain and one malt, as well as a blending plant, but since it was sold to its present owners, Destilerías y Crianza del Whisky SA, of Spain, it has concentrated production on this single malt. Most of the distillery's produce goes into blends.

VISITORS The distillery is open to visitors during the distilling season. Telephone 0674-72737.

LONG JOHN

Allied Distillers, Dumbarton,
Dunbartonshire

TYPE Blend

STRENGTH 40%, 43%

TASTE RATING 2–3

MINIATURES Yes

COMMENTS A medium-bodied blend with a very slight peaty tang to its pleasant, nicely rounded flavour.

BLENDERS The original company was founded by 'Long' John Macdonald, a statuesque man who built Ben Nevis Distillery at Fort William in 1823. The distillery had grain and malt stills, and its produce changed from a malt to a blend around the turn of the century. The company was bought by Chaplin, a London wine and spirit merchant in 1911, and they in turn were bought by the spirit merchants Seager, Evans in 1936. The company changed its name to Long John International in 1971 and, after several acquisitions, it is now operated by Allied Distillers.

VISITORS The plant is not suitable for visitors.

LONGMORN

Longmorn Distillery, Elgin, Moray

TYPE Single malt

BOTTLING AGE 12, 15 years

STRENGTH 40%, 43%

TASTE RATING 3–4

MINIATURES Yes

COMMENTS Another classic Speyside malt of great character, Longmorn is a full-bodied whisky with a clean, fragrant aroma and a nutty, sweet taste.

DISTILLERY The distillery was built by James Duff in 1894 and stands on the road between Elgin and Rothes. Longmorn, along with its sister distillery of Benriach, merged with The Glenlivet and Glen Grant Distilleries and Hill Thomson to form The Glenlivet Distillers. The company was purchased by Seagram in 1976.

VISITORS The distillery is not open to visitors.

LONGROW

Springbank Distillery,
Campbeltown, Argyllshire

TYPE Single malt

BOTTLING AGE 18 years

STRENGTH 46%

TASTE RATING 5

MINIATURES Yes

COMMENTS Longrow is a pungent malt whose production process, using only peat-dried barley, lends it a distinctive, peaty taste with an almost medicinal aroma, yet a complementary trace of sweetness.

DISTILLERY Springbank Distillery produces Longrow as a second malt, although there previously was a Longrow Distillery in the town; it was closed in the late 1800s.

VISITORS Springbank Distillery is open to visitors strictly by appointment. Telephone 0586-552085 to arrange.

THE MACALLAN

Macallan Distillery, Craigellachie,
Banffshire

TYPE Single malt

BOTTLING AGE 7, 10, 12, 18
25 years

STRENGTH 40%, 43%, 57%

TASTE RATING 3–4

MINIATURES Yes

COMMENTS Its rich, sherried aroma with a hint of peaches, its smooth, elegant flavour and its delightfully mellow sherry aftertaste make The Macallan one of the most popular of malts.

DISTILLERY The Macallan's distinctive richness of taste and colour derives in part from its ageing in sweet sherry casks, a traditional practice which this distillery is the only one to maintain through all its range. The distillery itself originated on a farm set above a ford over the Spey, used by drovers travelling south. It passed through several hands before being bought and extended in 1892 by Roderick Kemp, whose descendants still control the company. The whisky has been one of the best-selling single malts in Britain in the past ten years.

VISITORS Visitors are welcome by appointment on weekdays. Telephone 0340-871471.

MILLBURN

Millburn Distillery, Inverness, Inverness-shire

TYPE Single malt

BOTTLING AGE Varies

STRENGTH Varies

TASTE RATING 3–4

MINIATURES Yes

COMMENTS A rich Highland malt of medium-to-full body with a certain fruitiness in the palate and a balancing dry finish. Available from independent merchants.

DISTILLERY Millburn was one of the older Highland distilleries, being established around 1825, although distilling is said to have been carried out on the site as early as 1807. It was closed in 1985 and demolished three years later. This, added to the fact that its product is not available under the distillery label, makes it generally hard to find, and its malt will, of course, become rarer in future.

Established 1842

CADENHEAD'S

AUTHENTIC
COLLECTION

150th anniversary bottling

Single Malt Scotch Whisky

This whisky has been bottled from a selected individual cask
in its natural state and shows the character of that cask.
It has not been diluted with water. It has not been treated to
change its colour and is free from all additives. It has
not been subjected to any filtration that might remove
natural constituents and spoil its flavour.
It is the authentic product of its distillery.

Bottled by Wm. Cadenhead, 32 Union Street, Campbeltown,
SCOTLAND

From
MILLBURN
Distillery
Distilled December 1969 and bottled March 1992
Matured in an oak cask
for **22** years
Product of Scotland

70cl   51.7% vol

CONNOISSEURS
CHOICE

*Connoisseurs Choice, a
range of single malts from
various distilcts of
Scotland.*

*In the Highlands
are situated the greatest
number of malt whisky
distilleries.*

SINGLE HIGHLAND
MALT SCOTCH WHISKY
DISTILLED AT
MILLBURN
DISTILLERY
Proprietors: MacLan Duff (Distillers) Ltd

DISTILLED **1971** DISTILLED

SPECIALLY SELECTED, PRODUCED AND BOTTLED BY

GORDON & MACPHAIL
ELGIN · SCOTLAND
PRODUCT OF SCOTLAND

70cl   40% vol

181

MILTONDUFF

Miltonduff-Glenlivet Distillery,
Elgin, Moray

TYPE Single malt

BOTTLING AGE 12 years

STRENGTH 40%, 43%

TASTE RATING 2–3

MINIATURES Yes

COMMENTS A nice Speyside
malt, medium-bodied and
smooth, with a floral note.

DISTILLERY Miltonduff-Glenlivet Distillery stands just
south of Elgin near Pluscarden Abbey, and the distillery's
old washhouse was said to have been built on the site of
the abbey's brewery. The distillery was founded in 1824,
and draws its water from the nearby Black Burn which
flows down peaty Black Hill. Miltonduff was one of
the original Hiram Walker distilleries acquired in 1937
and today operates under their subsidiary, Allied
Distillers.

VISITORS Visitors are welcome by appointment.
Telephone 0343-547433 to arrange.

SPEYSIDE
SINGLE MALT
SCOTCH WHISKY

MORTLACH

was the first of seven
distilleries in *Dufftown.* In the
C19 farm animals kept in
adjoining byres were fed on
barley left over from processing
Today water from springs in
the *CONVAL HILLS* is used to
produce this delightful
smooth, fruity single
MALT SCOTCH WHISKY

A G E D **16** Y E A R S

Distilled & Bottled in *SCOTLAND*
MORTLACH DISTILLERY
Dufftown, Keith, Banffshire, Scotland

43% vol   70 cl

MORTLACH

Mortlach Distillery, Dufftown,
Keith, Banffshire

TYPE Single malt

BOTTLING AGE 16 years

STRENGTH 43%

TASTE RATING 4

MINIATURES Yes

COMMENTS A Speyside malt of
mellow, fruity flavour with a
definite peatiness and a dryness in
the finish.

DISTILLERY Another of
Dufftown's distilleries, this time
standing in a little valley outside
the town, by the River Dullan.
The distillery draws its water not
from the river but from springs in the local Conval Hills.
Founded in 1823, it was, in fact, the first of the
distilleries to be built in the capital of Speyside whisky-
making, and it enjoyed a monopoly in the town until
1887. The distillery has been modernized twice this
century and is now owned by United Distillers.

VISITORS Visitors are welcome by appointment.
Telephone 0340-20318 to arrange.

NORTH PORT

North Port Distillery,
Brechin, Angus

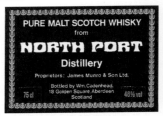

PURE MALT SCOTCH WHISKY
from
NORTH PORT
Distillery
Proprietors : James Munro & Son Ltd.
Bottled by Wm. Cadenhead,
18 Golden Square, Aberdeen
Scotland
75 cl   46% vol

TYPE Single malt

BOTTLING AGE Varies

STRENGTH Varies

TASTE RATING 2

MINIATURES Yes

COMMENTS Available from independent bottling merchants, North Port is a light-bodied, dry, fairly astringent whisky, best drunk as an aperitif.

DISTILLERY The older of the two distilleries in Brechin (Glencadam being the other), North Port was founded in 1820 by David Guthrie, a prominent Brechin businessman and local politician and managed by his sons from 1823; two brothers in the Guthrie family had interests in the whisky industry while a third, Thomas, was active in the Temperance movement. The distillery, latterly owned by the Distillers Company Ltd, was closed down in 1983 and sold in 1990.

OBAN

Oban Distillery, Oban, Argyllshire

TYPE Single malt

BOTTLING AGE 14 years

STRENGTH 43%

TASTE RATING 2–3

MINIATURES Yes

COMMENTS An intriguing, complex malt with a full Island character which is balanced by a soft Highland finish.

DISTILLERY First built as a brewery in 1794, Oban Distillery was the work of the Stevenson family, noted entrepreneurs and the founders of modern Oban at that time. The distillery, which stands at the harbour front, draws its water from the Ardconnel area of peaty uplands a mile from the town. It is licensed to John Hopkins, now owned by United Distillers.

VISITORS Visitors are welcome 0930–1700 Mon.–Fri. all year and 0930–1700 Sat., Easter–Oct. Telephone 0631-62110.

OLD FETTERCAIRN

Fettercairn Distillery, Fettercairn,
Laurencekirk, Kincardineshire

OLD FETTERCAIRN
ESTABLISHED 1824
10 YEARS OLD
SINGLE HIGHLAND MALT
SCOTCH WHISKY

Distilled, aged and bottled
in Scotland by
FETTERCAIRN DISTILLERS COMPANY
PRODUCT OF SCOTLAND

730ml   43% Alc/Vol
(86° Proof)

TYPE Single malt

BOTTLING AGE 10 years

STRENGTH 40%, 43%

TASTE RATING 3–4

MINIATURES Yes

COMMENTS A smooth single malt with a full, malty taste and a satisfyingly dry counterbalance.

DISTILLERY Fettercairn was another distillery, like North Port, to be founded by Brechin's Guthrie brothers. First established at its present location in 1824, Fettercairn Distillery is situated at the edge of the Grampian Mountains, from which it takes its spring-water supplies. The distillery, which was extended in 1966, was the first to use oil for heating its stills. It is presently owned by Whyte & Mackay.

VISITORS Visitors are welcome at the distillery's Visitor Centre 1000–1630 Mon.–Sat., May–Sept. Telephone 05614-205 to arrange group bookings.

OLD PARR

United Distillers, Banbeath,
Leven, Fife

TYPE De luxe

BOTTLING AGE 0, 12 years

STRENGTH 43%

TASTE RATING 2

MINIATURES No

COMMENTS A blend of fine
whiskies, with a smooth and
mellow taste and exceptional
depth of flavour.

BLENDERS The firm which produced Old Parr,
Macdonald Greenlees, is now owned by United
Distillers. The brand was first produced in the early
twentieth century by the Greenlees brothers from
Glasgow, and was aimed specifically at the southern
English market. After the First World War, the com-
pany amalgamated with Alexander & Macdonald of
Leith and William Williams of Aberdeen, owners of
Glendullan Distillery. The whole company joined the
Distillers Company Ltd in 1925. Most of the com-
pany's energies are directed into the production of Old
Parr, the bulk of which goes for export to Central and
South America, Japan and the Far East, where it is among
the most popular whiskies.

100 PIPERS

Chivas Brothers, Paisley

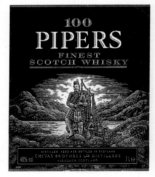

TYPE Blend

STRENGTH 40%

TASTE RATING 2

MINIATURES Yes

COMMENTS A smooth, mellow blend with light, malty flavours.

BLENDERS Legend has it that when you taste a good Scotch whisky you can hear pipers playing; two if the whisky is mild, three or four if it is smooth; five or six if it is mellow – all of which is said to indicate an exceptional Scotch whisky in 100 Pipers! 100 Pipers is one of several Seagram blends which include Passport, the de luxe Chivas Regal and the super-premium 21-year-old Royal Salute.

THE ORIGINAL MACKINLAY

Invergordon Distillers, Leith, Edinburgh

TYPE Blend

STRENGTH 40%

TASTE RATING 2

MINIATURES Yes

COMMENTS A well-balanced and nicely aged whisky with a smooth, malty aroma and a relatively full, lingering and slightly sweet flavour.

BLENDERS The success of the Mackinlay firm began under James, son of Charles Mackinlay, founder of the Leith company in 1824. The original Mackinlays blend appeared in 1850, and James was responsible for its success in the lucrative markets of southern England, gaining contracts to supply whisky to the House of Commons and to Ernest Shackleton's 1907 expedition to the South Pole. James Mackinlay was a co-founder of Glen Mhor Distillery, and bought Glen Albyn at the end of the nineteenth century; both were sold in 1972. Today, the company is part of the Invergordon Distillers Group. As well as The Original, the Mackinlay range also includes 12-year-old and 21-year-old blends.

VISITORS Visitors are accepted by appointment. Telephone 031-554 4404 to arrange.

PINWINNIE

Inver House Distillers, Moffat Distillery,
Airdrie, Lanarkshire

TYPE De luxe

STRENGTH 40%

TASTE RATING 2–3

MINIATURES Yes

COMMENTS A Lowland de luxe
blend, Pinwinnie is a very
smooth whisky, with sweet, fragrant notes and a nicely rounded
finish.

BLENDERS Pinwinnie's producers, Inver House, also
own Knockdhu (producing An Cnoc) and Speyburn-
Glenlivet distilleries. Blending is carried out at their
complex at Moffat on the outskirts of Airdrie, a converted former paper mill which also holds a grain
distillery.

VISITORS The distillery and plant is not open to visitors.

SPEYSIDE
SINGLE MALT
SCOTCH WHISKY

PITTYVAICH

distillery is situated in the
DULLAN GLEN on the outskirts
of Dufftown, near to the historic
Mortlach Church which dates back
to the 0th. The distillery draws
water from two nearby

springs - CONVALLEYS and
BALLIEMORE. Pittyvaich single
MALT SCOTCH WHISKY
has a perfumed, fruity
nose and a robust flavour with
a hint of spiciness.

AGED 12 YEARS

Distilled & Bottled in SCOTLAND
PITTYVAICH DISTILLERS
Dufftown, Keith, Banffshire, Scotland

43% vol 70cl

PITTYVAICH

Pittyvaich-Glenlivet Distillery, Dufftown,
Keith, Banffshire

TYPE Single malt

BOTTLING AGE 12 years

STRENGTH 43%

TASTE RATING 4

MINIATURES Yes

COMMENTS Pittyvaich is a
Speyside malt with a perfumed
fruitiness with a hint of spice and
a strong aftertaste.

DISTILLERY It was the success of
neighbouring Dufftown-Glenlivet
and the quality of its water supply,
from the local Jock's Well, which
encouraged Bell's to build the brand-new Pittyvaich-
Glenlivet Distillery almost next door, in 1974. Almost
all of its product now goes into United Distillers' blends,
although some of the single malt is marketed under the
distillery's own label. In 1993 this distillery was earmarked for closure by United Distillers.

VISITORS Visitors are welcome by appointment.
Telephone 0340-20561 to arrange.

PORT ELLEN

Port Ellen Distillery, Port Ellen,
Islay, Argyllshire

TYPE Single malt

BOTTLING AGE Varies

STRENGTH Varies

TASTE RATING 3–4

MINIATURES Yes

COMMENTS A milder Islay
than some, Port Ellen is a
basically dry malt with a reasonably mild, peaty flavour.
Available from independent bottling merchants.

Established 1842

CADENHEAD'S

AUTHENTIC
COLLECTION
150th anniversary bottling
Single Malt Scotch Whisky

This whisky has been bottled from a selected individual cask
in its natural state and shows the character of that cask.
It has not been diluted with water. It has not been treated to
change its colour and is free from all additives. It has
not been subjected to any filtration that might remove
natural constituents and spoil the flavour.
It is the authentic product of its distillery.

Bottled by Wm. Cadenhead, 32 Union Street, Campbeltown,
SCOTLAND

From
PORT ELLEN
Distillery
Distilled April 1981 and bottled March 1992
Matured in an oak cask
for **10** years

70cl   Product of Scotland   64% vol

DISTILLERY Port Ellen was established in 1824 and
stands in the town of the same name in the south of the
island. The distillery was closed earlier this century,
from 1930 until 1967, when it was modernized and
enlarged. The distillery was mothballed in 1984 and is
presently owned by United Distillers.

PRIDE OF THE LOWLANDS

Gordon and MacPhail, Elgin, Moray

TYPE Vatted malt

BOTTLING AGE 12 years

STRENGTH 40%

TASTE RATING 2

MINIATURES Yes

COMMENTS One of Gordon and MacPhail's series of malts capturing the classic characteristics of the leading regions, this is a vatting of the finest whiskies distilled in the Lowlands, and has a sweet, butterscotch-like nose with a smoky–woody finish.

PRODUCERS Gordon and MacPhail's premises are located in Elgin on the banks of the River Lossie and close to Speyside, arguably the heart of the Scotch whisky industry. The firm has been in business for almost a century, initially as a licensed grocers and wine and spirit merchants. Their business encompasses the vatting, blending and bottling of whiskies, while their retail shop is among the leading malt whisky shops in the UK.

VISITORS Gordon and MacPhail's shop, South St, Elgin is open 0900–1715 Mon.–Wed. (0900–1300 Wed. in winter), 0830–1715 Thu.–Fri., 0900–1700 Sat.

PRIDE OF ISLAY

Gordon and MacPhail, Elgin, Moray

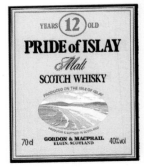

TYPE Vatted malt

BOTTLING AGE 12 years

STRENGTH 40%

TASTE RATING 4

MINIATURES Yes

COMMENTS One of Gordon and MacPhail's series of malts capturing the classic characteristics of the leading regions, this is a vatting of the finest whiskies produced on Islay. It has a complex nose with salty, medicinal and smoky flavours.

PRODUCERS Gordon and MacPhail started in business in 1895 as a licensed grocers and wine and spirit merchant, as had done so many of the foremost names among the Scotch whisky blending industry. Unlike the others, however, Gordon and MacPhail have retained all the original aspects of their business as well as extending into vatting, blending and bottling, and they are today the world's leading malt whisky specialists.

VISITORS Gordon and MacPhail's shop, South St, Elgin is open 0900–1715 Mon.–Wed. (0900–1300 Wed. in winter), 0830–1715 Thu.–Fri., 0900–1700 Sat.

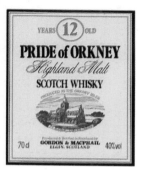

PRIDE OF ORKNEY

Gordon and MacPhail, Elgin, Moray

TYPE Vatted malt

BOTTLING AGE 12 years

STRENGTH 40%, 43%, 57%

TASTE RATING 3

MINIATURES Yes

COMMENTS One of Gordon and MacPhail's series of malts capturing the classic characteristics of the leading regions, this is a vatting of the finest whiskies produced in Orkney, and is a well-balanced whisky with a sweet, toasted nose, with a hint of heather.

PRODUCERS Gordon and MacPhail's premises are located in Elgin on the banks of the River Lossie and close to Speyside, arguably the heart of the Scotch whisky industry. The firm has been in business for almost a century, initially as a licensed grocers and wine and spirit merchants. Their business encompasses the vatting, blending and bottling of whiskies, while their retail shop is among the leading malt whisky shops in the UK.

VISITORS Gordon and MacPhail's shop, South St, Elgin is open 0900–1715 Mon.–Wed. (0900–1300 Wed. in winter), 0830–1715 Thu.–Fri., 0900–1700 Sat.

PRIDE OF STRATHSPEY

Gordon and MacPhail, Elgin, Moray

TYPE Vatted malt

BOTTLING AGE 12, 25 years

STRENGTH 40%

TASTE RATING 2

MINIATURES Yes

COMMENTS One of Gordon
and MacPhail's series of malts
capturing the classic characteristics of the leading regions,
this is a vatting of the finest whiskies distilled in
Strathspey. This malt is a citrus-fruity whisky in nose and
palate, with a very pleasant aftertaste.

PRODUCERS Gordon and MacPhail started in business
in 1895 as a licensed grocers and wine and spirit merchant, as had done so many of the foremost names
among the Scotch whisky blending industry. Unlike the
others, however, Gordon and MacPhail have retained all
the original aspects of their business as well as extending
into vatting, blending and bottling, and they are today
the world's leading malt whisky specialists.

VISITORS Gordon and MacPhail's shop, South St, Elgin
is open 0900–1715 Mon.–Wed. (0900–1300 Wed. in
winter), 0830–1715 Thu.–Fri., 0900–1700 Sat.

PULTENEY

Pulteney Distillery,
Wick, Caithness

PURE MALT SCOTCH WHISKY
from

PULTENEY
Distillery

Proprietors: Pulteney Distillery Co. Ltd.

75 cl   Bottled by Wm. Cadenhead,
         18 Golden Square, Aberdeen   46% vol
         Scotland

TYPE Single malt

BOTTLING AGE Varies

STRENGTH Varies

TASTE RATING 3–4

MINIATURES Yes

COMMENTS Reputedly one of the fastest-maturing whiskies, Pulteney is a distinctive malt with a pungent aroma and salty tang underlain by peaty notes, perhaps due to the exposed coastal position of the distillery. Available from independent bottlers.

DISTILLERY Pulteney Distillery was established in 1826 in a new district of Wick which had been built to accommodate workers from the local herring industry, and in such a situation it had a ready market. It was closed during the slump of the 1920s and was not reopened until 1951, being sold to James & George Stodart Ltd of Dumbarton, a Hiram Walker subsidiary, four years later. It is still owned by the Hiram Walker Group and operates under their subsidiary, Allied Distillers. The distillery is near the ruins of the four-teenth-century Castle Oliphant, known as the Auld Man o' Wick.

VISITORS The distillery has no reception centre but visitors are welcome by appointment. Telephone 0955-2371 to arrange.

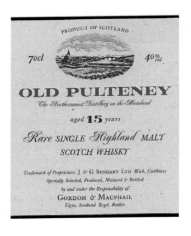

LOWLAND SINGLE MALT SCOTCH WHISKY

Established on its present site at CAMELON in 1840

ROSEBANK

distillery stands on the banks of the FORTH and CLYDE CANAL. This was once a busy thoroughfare with boats and steamers continually passing by; it is still the source of water for cooling. This single MALT SCOTCH WHISKY is triple distilled which accounts for its light distinctive nose and well balanced flavour.

AGED **12** YEARS

Distilled & Bottled in SCOTLAND
ROSEBANK DISTILLERY
Falkirk · Stirlingshire · Scotland

43% vol 70cl

ROSEBANK

Rosebank Distillery, Camelon, Falkirk, Stirlingshire

TYPE Single malt

BOTTLING AGE 12 years

STRENGTH 43%

TASTE RATING 2

MINIATURES Yes

COMMENTS One of the best known Lowland malts, Rosebank is a smooth, mild whisky of light and subtle character, which makes it ideal as a pre-dinner dram.

DISTILLERY Although a distillery was operating on this site in 1817, the present buildings generally date from 1840 when much rebuilding took place. It stands on the banks of the Forth and Clyde Canal, on the outskirts of Falkirk. Triple distillation processes are used at Rosebank, which has one wash still and two spirit stills. In 1993 this distillery was earmarked for closure by United Distillers.

VISITORS The distillery is not open to visitors.

ROYAL BRACKLA

Royal Brackla Distillery,
Cawdor, Nairnshire

TYPE Single malt

BOTTLING AGE
          10 years

STRENGTH 43%

TASTE RATING 4

MINIATURES Yes

COMMENTS A light, fresh, grassy malt with a hint of fruitiness. This single malt can be difficult to find.

DISTILLERY Brackla Distillery's produce has been allowed to call itself 'Royal' since 1838, when Queen Victoria granted it a Royal Warrant. Founded in 1812, the distillery has been rebuilt and extended several times in the past two centuries, although it is currently moth-balled. It is licensed to Bissets, now owned by United Distillers, and almost all of its produce goes into their blends.

VISITORS Visitors are welcome by appointment. Telephone 06677-280.

Established 1842

CADENHEAD'S

AUTHENTIC COLLECTION

150th anniversary bottling

Single Malt Scotch Whisky

This whisky has been bottled from a selected individual cask
in its natural state and shows the character of that cask.
It has not been diluted with water. It has not been treated to
change its colour and is free from all additives. It has
not been vat/wshed to any filtration that might remove
natural constituents and spoil its flavour.
It is the authentic product of its distillery.

Bottled by Wm. Cadenhead, 32 Union Street, Campbeltown.
SCOTLAND

From
ROYAL BRACKLA
Distillery

Distilled February 1966 and bottled March 1992
Matured in an oak cask
for **26** years
70cl   Product of Scotland   56.9% vol

CONNOISSEURS CHOICE

*Connoisseurs Choice, a
range of single malts from
various distins of
Scotland*

*In the Highlands
are situated the greater
number of malt whisky
distilleries.*

SINGLE HIGHLAND
MALT SCOTCH WHISKY
ROYAL BRACKLA
DISTILLERY
Proprietors: John Bisset & Co. Ltd

DISTILLED **1976** DISTILLED

SPECIALLY SELECTED, PRODUCED AND BOTTLED BY

70cl   GORDON & MACPHAIL   40%vol
ELGIN · SCOTLAND
PRODUCT OF SCOTLAND

201

ROYAL CULROSS

Gibson International, Glasgow

TYPE Vatted malt

BOTTLING AGE 8 years

STRENGTH 40%

TASTE RATING 3–4

MINIATURES Yes

COMMENTS Royal Culross is a vatted malt of substantial character and body with a pungent aroma and smooth, malty tones balanced by a lighter, slightly peaty edge.

BLENDERS Royal Culross is one of a range of whiskies associated with the Glen Scotia Distillery in Campbeltown. It is produced by Gibson International, a company with widespread interests in the whisky industry, from distilling to exporting. The company was formed in 1988 to control, develop and promote their two distilleries (Glen Scotia and Littlemill) and associated blends. As well as its whiskies, Gibson International also has other interests in the spirits industry.

ROYAL LOCHNAGAR

*Royal Lochnagar Distillery,
Crathie, Ballater, Aberdeenshire*

TYPE Single malt

BOTTLING AGE 12 years, no age given for Selected Reserve

STRENGTH 40%, 43% (Selected Reserve)

TASTE RATING 3–4

MINIATURES Yes

COMMENTS A big-bodied, rich and highly fruity malt with a delightfully sherried flavour. Royal Lochnagar Selected Reserve, with a more robust taste, is also available.

DISTILLERY Built by James Robertson in 1826 on the slopes of the mountain from which it took its name, this distillery was destroyed by fire (reputedly the work of rival illicit distillers) in 1841 before being taken over and rebuilt by John Begg four years later. The 'Royal' prefix came after a visit and tasting in 1848 by Queen Victoria (said to be partial to whisky), who was staying at nearby Balmoral. The distillery was bought by Dewar's, is now owned by United Distillers and is licensed to John Begg Ltd.

VISITORS Visitors are welcome 1000–1700 Mon.–Fri
all year and 1000–1700 Sat., 1100–1600 Sun.,
Easter–Oct. Telephone 03397-42273.

ST MAGDALENE

*St Magdalene Distillery,
Linlithgow, West Lothian*

TYPE Single malt

BOTTLING AGE Varies

STRENGTH Varies

TASTE RATING 2–3

MINIATURES Yes

COMMENTS A light-bodied
Lowland malt, smooth and
generally dry yet with a hint
of fruity sweetness. Available
only from independent merchants, its produce can be
difficult to find.

DISTILLERY St Magdalene, built on the lands of St
Mary's Cross towards the end of the nineteenth century, was until recently the sole survivor of the six
distilleries which existed in Linlithgow in the last century.
Linlithgow had been a centre of brewing and distilling
due to an abundance of barley and fine water from local
supplies. It was closed by United Distillers, its owners,
in the mid 1980s, the building subsequently being converted to private housing.

SCAPA

Scapa Distillery, Kirkwall, Orkney

TYPE Single malt

BOTTLING AGE Varies

STRENGTH Varies

TASTE RATING 3

MINIATURES Yes

COMMENTS Scapa, available only from independent bottlers, is a medium-bodied malt with a dryish, heathery flavour which is complemented by a satisfyingly malty sweetness.

DISTILLERY Scapa is one of two distilleries in Kirkwall (Highland Park being the other), yet despite their proximity, their whiskies taste quite different. Scapa was built in 1885 by Macfarlane and Townsend (the latter already a well-known distiller on Speyside) and was bought by Hiram Walker in 1954. It is now licensed to their subsidiary, Allied Distillers. The distillery overlooks Scapa Flow where the German fleet was scuttled during the First World War.

VISITORS The distillery has no reception centre, but visitors are welcome by appointment. Telephone 0856-872071 to arrange.

40% VOL

Product of Scotland

70cl

SCAPA

SINGLE HIGHLAND MALT

SCOTCH WHISKY

Distilled 1979 Distilled

Trademark of Proprietors

TAYLOR & FERGUSON LTD · SCAPA · ORKNEY

SPECIALLY SELECTED, PRODUCED, MATURED & BOTTLED BY
AND UNDER THE RESPONSIBILITY OF

Gordon & Macphail

THON SCOTLAND 15660 BOTTLES

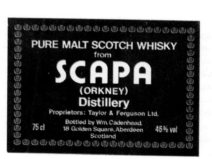

PURE MALT SCOTCH WHISKY
from

SCAPA

(ORKNEY)
Distillery

Proprietors: Taylor & Ferguson Ltd.

Bottled by Wm. Cadenhead,
18 Golden Square, Aberdeen
Scotland

75 cl   46% vol

207

SCOTIA ROYALE

Gibson International,
Glasgow

TYPE De luxe

BOTTLING AGE 12 years

STRENGTH 40%, 43%

TASTE RATING 2–3

MINIATURES Yes

COMMENTS A medium-bodied de luxe blend, Scotia
Royale is a smooth, well-balanced whisky with a hint
of peat. Glen Scotia malt is one of this whisky's most
important ingredients.

BLENDERS Scotia Royale is one of a range of whiskies
associated with the Glen Scotia Distillery in
Campbeltown. It is produced by Gibson International,
a company with widespread interests in the whisky
industry, from distilling to exporting. The company
was formed in 1988 to control, develop and promote
their two distilleries (Glen Scotia and Littlemill) and
the associated blends. As well as its whiskies, Gibson
International also has other interests in the spirits
industry.

THE
SINGLETON
OF AUCHROISK

Auchroisk Distillery, Mulben, Banffshire

TYPE Single malt

BOTTLING AGE Minimum 10 years

STRENGTH 40%

TASTE RATING 2–3

MINIATURES Yes

COMMENTS This whisky has won eight major awards in the six years since its introduction to the market in 1987. It is medium bodied, with a hint of peat to its flavour, which is smooth and sweet, derived from part-maturation in sherry casks.

DISTILLERY One of the newest Scottish distilleries (opened in 1974), Auchroisk has been marketing its single malt for only the past few years. It was built by International Distillers and Vintners. Dorie's Well provides the distillery with its pure, natural water source. The building itself has won several awards, including one from the Angling Foundation for not interfering with the upriver progress of local salmon.

VISITORS Visitors are welcome by appointment on weekdays. Telephone 0542-6333 to arrange.

SPEYBURN

Speyburn-Glenlivet Distillery,
Rothes, Moray

TYPE Single malt

BOTTLING AGE 10 years

STRENGTH 40%

TASTE RATING 3–4

MINIATURES Yes

COMMENTS A medium-bod-
ied whisky with a firm yet
subtle flavour and a dry,
warming, peaty finish.

DISTILLERY Speyburn was built in 1897 on the outskirts of Rothes, and is one of the most picturesque
distilleries in Scotland. Originally built for the blenders
John Hopkins, it was acquired in 1992 by Inver House
Distillers.

VISITORS The distillery is not open to visitors.

SPRINGBANK

Springbank Distillery,
Campbeltown, Argyllshire

TYPE Single malt

BOTTLING AGE 12, 15, 21, 25, 30 years.

STRENGTH 46%

TASTE RATING 4

MINIATURES Yes

COMMENTS Often described as a classic malt, Springbank is a smooth, mellow whisky, light yet complex and full-flavoured.

DISTILLERY Springbank was built in 1828 by the Mitchell family, previous owners of an illicit still in the area. The distillery is still owned today by the founders' family, and has never been closed at any time in its history. Along with Glenfiddich, it is unusual in bottling its own malt on the premises, and is also the only distillery in Scotland to carry out the full process of malt whisky production, from floor malting to bottling. Springbank is not coloured with caramel, and is the only malt available under a distillery label which has not been chill filtered. Longrow single malt is also produced here.

VISITORS The distillery is open to visitors strictly by appointment. Telephone 0586-552085 to arrange.

STAG'S BREATH LIQUEUR

Meikles of Scotland, Newtonmore, Inverness-shire

TYPE Liqueur

STRENGTH 19.8%

TASTE RATING 2

MINIATURES Yes

COMMENTS A light and smooth union of fine Speyside whisky with fermented comb honey. Equally suited to a role as an aperitif or as a digestif.

BLENDERS Meikles of Scotland is a small Speyside family firm and has been producing Stag's Breath since 1989. The liqueur takes its name from one of the fictional whiskies lost at sea in Sir Compton Mackenzie's famous re-telling of the sinking of the *SS Politician*, in his book, *Whisky Galore*.

VISITORS There are no visitor facilities at present.

STEWART'S CREAM OF THE BARLEY

Allied Distillers, Dumbarton, Dunbartonshire

TYPE Blend

STRENGTH 40%

TASTE RATING 2

MINIATURES Yes

COMMENTS A popular and good-quality blend with a soft and well-balanced, sweetish, malty flavour.

BLENDERS Stewart & Son of Dundee was founded in 1831 and was one of the first companies to exploit newer methods of distilling – particularly the new patent still – and the beginnings of the market for blended whiskies. The company grew steadily in size and the brand in popularity. It was bought by Allied-Lyons in 1969 and today operates under Allied Distillers.

VISITORS The plant is not suitable for visitors.

EST 1831

RARE SELECTED

STEWARTS
CREAM OF THE
BARLEY

BLENDED SCOTCH WHISKY

DISTILLED BLENDED & BOTTLED IN SCOTLAND
STEWART & SON OF DUNDEE LIMITED
DUNDEE SCOTLAND
100% SCOTCH WHISKIES

40% vol   70 cl

AGED **12** YEARS

Strathisla

Pure Highland Malt Scotch Whisky

Distilled and Bottled by:
CHIVAS BROTHERS LIMITED
STRATHISLA DISTILLERY,
KEITH, SCOTLAND

40% vol   75 cl

STRATHISLA

Strathisla Distillery, Keith, Banffshire

TYPE Single malt

BOTTLING AGE 12 years

STRENGTH 40%

TASTE RATING 4

MINIATURES Yes

COMMENTS A big, robust whisky, full-flavoured and fruity, with a sherried sweetness.

DISTILLERY According to records, production of a 'heather ale' by local clerics had been taking place in this area as early as 1208. The later siting of Milton Distillery (as Strathisla was formerly known) here in 1708 may have been for the same reasons: set in a good barley-producing area, it also had easy access to a pure local spring which had been a holy well of local Cistercian monks, and which is said to be guarded by water spirits. The distillery, one of the oldest and most picturesque in the Highlands, passed through several hands until it was bought by Chivas Brothers, a Seagram subsidiary, in 1950.

VISITORS The distillery is on the Whisky Trail and visitors are welcome 0900–1630 Mon.–Fri., Easter–end Sept. Telephone 05422-7471.

TALISKER

*Talisker Distillery, Carbost,
Isle of Skye, Inverness-shire*

TYPE Single malt

BOTTLING AGE 8, 10 years

STRENGTH 45.8%

TASTE RATING 5

MINIATURES Yes

COMMENTS Talisker is Skye's only malt and has been described as being mid-way between Islay and Highland malts. It is full-bodied with a rich, peaty flavour and elements of malty, fruity sweetness. It was praised by R. L. Stevenson in his poem, *The Scotsman's Return from Abroad*, as one of 'The King o' drinks'.

DISTILLERY Talisker Distillery had an inauspicious start in the 1830s, being denounced by a local minister as a great curse for the area. Despite his disapproval, distilling has continued successfully, with the distillery changing hands several times. A victim of several fires throughout its 160-year history, it was totally rebuilt in 1960. The distillery is owned today by United Distillers, and some of its product goes into Johnnie Walker blends.

VISITORS Visitors are welcome 0930–1630 Mon.–Fri., Apr.–Oct., and by appointment 1400–1630 Nov.–Mar. Telephone 047842-203.

216

TAMDHU

Tamdhu-Glenlivet Distillery,
Knockando, Aberlour, Banffshire

TYPE Single malt

BOTTLING AGE 10, 15 years

STRENGTH 40%, 43%

TASTE RATING 3–4

MINIATURES Yes

COMMENTS A good, smooth Speyside malt, which is slightly peaty but has a delicate sweetness.

DISTILLERY Highland Distilleries bought this distillery shortly after it opened in 1897 and have owned it ever since. It was extensively refurbished in the 1970s and is now one of the most modern on Speyside, with the additional feature of a viewing gallery from which visitors can see the whisky-making processes. The former train station, at the distillery entrance, has been converted into a shop and visitor reception area.

VISITORS The distillery is on the Whisky Trail and visitors are welcome 1000–1600 Mon.–Sat., June–end Sept., Mon.–Fri. 6 Apr.–June, or by appointment. Large parties should telephone in advance. Telephone 03406-221.

TAMNAVULIN-GLENLIVET

*Tamnavulin-Glenlivet Distillery,
Tomnavoulin, Banffshire*

TYPE Single malt

BOTTLING AGE 10 years

STRENGTH 40%

TASTE RATING 3

MINIATURES Yes

COMMENTS A lightish, mellow
Glenlivet-type malt with a sweetish bouquet and taste but an
underlying smoky note.

DISTILLERY Opened in 1966, this is one of the newest
Highland distilleries. It is a rather functional building, set
on slopes above the River Livet and using water from a
nearby burn. The visitor centre, which was recently
opened, however, is much more picturesque, built in an
old watermill.

VISITORS The distillery is on the Whisky Trail and
visitors are welcome 0930–1600 (last complete tour
1545) Mon.–Sat., 23 Mar.–30 Oct.; or by appointment. Large parties should telephone in advance.
Telephone 08073-442.

TEACHER'S HIGHLAND CREAM

Allied Distillers, Dumbarton,
Dunbartonshire

TYPE Blend

STRENGTH 40%, 43%

TASTE RATING 2

MINIATURES Yes

COMMENTS Teacher's Highland Cream is a superior blend which has a smooth, sweet flavour with a trace of dryer, heathery notes. It is one of the most popular blended whiskies in the UK. Its sister blend is the 12-year-old Teacher's Royal Highland.

BLENDERS The Teacher's company was begun in Glasgow in the 1830s by William Teacher, a young man barely in his twenties. The business started with licensed premises where people could drink whisky, and expanded through the years of the nineteenth century to include blending, bottling and export interests. Highland Cream was first marketed in 1884, although Teacher's

TEACHER'S HIGHLAND CREAM
cont.

did not build its first distillery, at Ardmore, until 1898.
The company has since concentrated on blending,
bottling and exporting, selling off its licensed shops.

VISITORS The plant is not suitable for visitors.

HIGHLAND
SINGLE MALT
SCOTCH WHISKY

The *Cromarty Firth* is one of the few places in the British Isles inhabited by *PORPOISE*. They can be seen quite regularly, & swimming close to the shore & less than a mile from

TEANINICH

distillery founded in 1817 in the *Ross-shire* town of ALNESS, the distillery is now one of the largest in Scotland. TEANINICH is an assertive single MALT WHISKY with a spicy, & smoky, satisfying taste.

AGED **10** YEARS

Distilled & Bottled in SCOTLAND
TEANINICH DISTILLERIES,
Alness, Ross-shire, Scotland

43% vol · 70 cl

CONNOISSEURS
CHOICE

Connoisseurs Choice, a range of single malts from various districts of Scotland

In the Highlands are situated the greatest number of malt whisky distilleries

SINGLE HIGHLAND
MALT SCOTCH WHISKY
DISTILLED AT
TEANINICH
Distillery
Proprietors R. H. Thomson & Co. (Distillers) Ltd.
DISTILLED **1982** DISTILLED

SPECIALLY SELECTED PRODUCED AND BOTTLED BY
GORDON & MACPHAIL
ELGIN SCOTLAND
PRODUCT OF SCOTLAND

70 cl · 40% vol

TEANINICH

Teaninich Distillery, Alness, Ross-shire

TYPE Single malt

BOTTLING AGE 10 years

STRENGTH 40%, 43%

TASTE RATING 3

MINIATURES Yes

COMMENTS A hard-to-find single malt, Teaninich is assertive with a spicy, smoky and satisfying taste.

DISTILLERY Teaninich Distillery dates from the early 1800s, although it was largely rebuilt in 1970 when a new distillery (known as the A-side) was constructed in front of the original (then known as the B-side). It is now owned by United Distillers, and most of the output goes for blending. It reopened in May 1990 after being mothballed for several years.

VISITORS Visitors are accepted by appointment.
Telephone 0349-882461 to arrange.

TOBERMORY

Tobermory Distillery, Tobermory, Mull, Argyllshire

TYPE Pure malt

BOTTLING AGE No age given

STRENGTH 40%

TASTE RATING 3

MINIATURES Yes

COMMENTS A nicely balanced, light malt with a delicate, flowery aroma and drier, heathery tones in its flavour. A good pre-dinner dram.

DISTILLERY Set in a wooded site by the sea, Tobermory Distillery has enjoyed mixed fortunes since it was first established in 1823. It has been closed several times during its existence, most recently in the 1980s when it was mothballed. Having reopened in 1990, the distillery is now back in production. The distillery was previously known as Ledaig, changing its name in the 1970s. It is one of the few family-owned independent distilleries.

VISITORS The Visitor Centre and Distillery Shop are open Mon.–Fri., Easter–30 Sept. Tours can be arranged at other times in the year. Telephone 0688-2119.

TOMATIN

Tomatin Distillery, Tomatin, Inverness-shire

TYPE Single malt

BOTTLING AGE 10, 12, 25 years

STRENGTH 40%, 43%

TASTE RATING 2

MINIATURES Yes

COMMENTS A light, clean malt, mild rather than strongly flavoured, with a pleasant, peaty note. A good aperitif.

DISTILLERY Standing over 1000 feet up in the Monadhliath Mountains, twelve miles south of Inverness, Tomatin has the misfortune of suffering occasional water shortages in dry years. It was built originally on the site of a fifteenth century distillery but, after modernization at the turn of this century, it became the largest-capacity distillery in the country, with production as high as five million gallons per annum. The company declined in the 1980s and went into receivership, but was bought by the Japanese firms of Takara Schuzo and Okura, thus becoming the first Scotch whisky distillery to be acquired by Japanese owners.

VISITORS Visitors are welcome 0930–1630 Mon.–Fri., Apr.–Aug., & 0930–1230 Sat., July–Aug. Large parties should telephone in advance. Telephone 08082-234.

TOMINTOUL-GLENLIVET

Tomintoul-Glenlivet Distillery,
Ballindalloch, Banffshire

TYPE Single malt

BOTTLING AGE 12 years

STRENGTH 40%, 43%

TASTE RATING 2–3

MINIATURES Yes

COMMENTS A light, delicate whisky with a fine balance of flavours in the Glenlivet style. An ideal dram for beginners, or as an aperitif.

DISTILLERY Built in 1965 in Tomintoul, the second-highest village in Scotland, Tomintoul-Glenlivet is also, at 1100 feet, one of the highest distilleries in the country. Water is drawn from the nearby Ballantruan spring.

VISITORS The distillery is not open to visitors.

TORMORE

The Tormore Distillery, Advie,
Grantown-on-Spey, Moray

TYPE Single malt

BOTTLING AGE 10 years

STRENGTH 40%, 43%

TASTE RATING 2–3

MINIATURES Yes

COMMENTS A medium-
bodied whisky, rich and
slightly nutty in flavour.
An after-dinner dram.

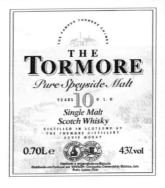

DISTILLERY This was the first new distillery to be built
on Speyside this century. It is in a pleasant setting, is
attractive-looking, and has the delightfully kitsch touch
of a chiming clock which plays the air *Highland Laddie*
every hour. Tormore's water comes from the Achvochkie
Burn, fed by the nearby Loch an Oir (Lake of Gold). An
impressive working model of Tormore Distillery can
be seen at the Scotch Whisky Heritage Centre in
Edinburgh's Royal Mile. The distillery itself is owned by
Allied Distillers.

VISITORS Visitors are welcome by appointment.
Telephone 08075-244 to arrange.

226

TULLIBARDINE

Tullibardine Distillery,
Blackford, Perthshire

PRODUCT OF SCOTLAND

A Single Malt Scotch Whisky of quality
and distinction distilled and bottled by
TULLIBARDINE DISTILLERY LIMITED
BLACKFORD   PERTHSHIRE   SCOTLAND

40%vol   70cl

TYPE Single malt

BOTTLING AGE 10 years

STRENGTH 40%

TASTE RATING 2–3

MINIATURES Yes

COMMENTS Tullibardine is a good, all-round single malt, full-bodied, and with a sweet, well-rounded flavour with a grapey note.

DISTILLERY Tullibardine Distillery was built on the site of a medieval brewery reputed to have produced ale for the coronation of James IV in 1488. It was opened as a distillery in 1949 and is actually situated at Blackford, a few miles away from Tullibardine village.

VISITORS Visitors are welcome by appointment on weekday afternoons. Telephone 076482-252 to arrange.

VAT 69

United Distillers, Kilmarnock, Ayrshire

TYPE Blend

STRENGTH 40%

TASTE RATING 2

MINIATURES Yes

COMMENTS A smooth, well-balanced and distinctly mature blend, light but with a pleasantly malty background.

BLENDERS Sandersons were Leith wine and spirit merchants who moved into whisky blending in the 1860s. William Sanderson was keen to find a notable blend to market and produced 100 different whiskies to be tested, each in numbered casks. The unanimous choice of his associates was the whisky from vat number 69, and so the name suggested itself. It was introduced onto the market in 1882, and William Sanderson's son was responsible for early advertising and marketing successes. Sanderson was also a founder of the North British Distillery company in 1885, ensuring supplies of good grain whisky for his blends. Today Sanderson and its brands are owned by United Distillers.

WHITE HORSE

United Distillers, Glasgow

TYPE Blend

STRENGTH 40%

TASTE RATING 2–3

MINIATURES Yes

COMMENTS White Horse is a smooth and distinctive whisky with peaty elements in both its aroma and flavour. It is the leading standard blend in Japan.

BLENDERS White Horse Distillers, known until 1924 as Mackie & Co., was established by James Logan Mackie in 1861. The company became successful under its second head, Peter Mackie, entrepreneur and the driving force who registered the name 'White Horse', called after a famous Edinburgh coaching inn, for his blend in 1890. By the time he died in 1924 his whisky was one of the foremost blends in the world. Three years later White Horse Distillers joined the Distillers Company Ltd, with whom Mackie had had difficult relations during his lifetime. White Horse also produce Logan and White Horse Extra Fine, de luxe blends for the export market.

WHYTE & MACKAY SPECIAL RESERVE

Whyte & Mackay, Glasgow

TYPE Blend

STRENGTH 40%

TASTE RATING 2

MINIATURES Yes

COMMENTS A good quality, smooth, light-bodied whisky with a well-rounded, mellow sweetness which is said to come from the particular blending process the company uses.

BLENDERS James Whyte and Charles Mackay, both whisky merchants, began their partnership and blending firm in 1882. Sales and the company expanded steadily throughout the late nineteenth century and into the twentieth, although their main markets were always overseas. The company merged with Dalmore Distillery, with whom it had had a long-standing relationship, in the 1960s, and acquired two more distilleries, Fettercairn and Tomintoul-Glenlivet, after a merger with Sir Hugh Fraser's Scottish & Universal Investments Ltd in 1972. Whyte & Mackay went to Lonrho in 1979. The blending process which is said to add character to the Whyte & Mackay whiskies involves vatting the component malts together in sherry butts for at least six months,

then adding the grain content and leaving the resulting blend to mature further. Whyte & Mackay also produce 12-year-old and 21-year-old blends.

WILLIAM GRANT'S FAMILY RESERVE

Girvan Distillery, Girvan, Ayrshire

TYPE Blend

STRENGTH 40%

TASTE RATING 2

MINIATURES Yes

COMMENTS A traditional yet individual blend of smooth character with a light, fresh taste which incorporates elements of Glenfiddich and The Balvenie.

BLENDERS The Grants of Glenfiddich, producers of the world's biggest-selling single malt whisky, are responsible for the production of two blends: William Grant's Family Reserve and Grant's 12 Year Old, the latter being a de luxe blend. The company began as malt whisky distillers in 1887 at Glenfiddich, moving into blending and exporting in 1898 after Pattison, one of the largest blenders and wholesale merchants, and Grant's biggest buyers, went bankrupt. In 1962 the company built a large complex at Girvan, housing a grain distillery, a malt distillery (Ladyburn, now dismantled), and blending facilities. Blended products are bottled at a site in Paisley.

VISITORS The plant is not open to visitors.

INDEX OF MALT WHISKIES
BY PRODUCING REGION

ISLANDS

ISLAY

LOWLANDS

COLLINS GEM

Other Gem titles that may interest you include:

Gem Wine
An A-Z guide to the wines of the world featuring over 1800 wine terms, all clearly explained **£3.50**

Gem Clans and Tartans
Over 100 Scottish tartans illustrated in colour, with histories of their clans **£3.50**

Gem Flags
Up-to-date, full-colour guide to over 200 flags of the world, explaining their origins, history and significance **£3.50**

Gem Kings and Queens
Comprehensive coverage of the history, traditions and institutions of the British monarchy **£3.50**

Gem Ready Reference
A unique compilation of information from the world of measures, with quick reference conversion tables and helpful illustrations **£2.99**

COLLINS GEM

Bestselling Collins Gem titles include:

Gem English Dictionary (£3.50)
Gem Calorie Counter (£2.99)
Gem Thesaurus (£2.99)
Gem French Dictionary (£3.50)
Gem German Dictionary (£3.50)
Gem Basic Facts Mathematics (£2.99)
Gem Birds (£3.50)
Gem Babies' Names (£3.50)
Gem Card Games (£3.50)
Gem Atlas of the World (£3.50)

All Collins Gems are available from your local bookseller or can be ordered direct from the publishers.

In the UK, contact Mail Order, Dept 2M, HarperCollins Publishers, Westerhill Rd, Bishopbriggs, Glasgow, G64 2QT, listing the titles required and enclosing a cheque or p.o. for the value of the books plus £1.00 for the first title and 25p for each additional title to cover p&p. Access and Visa cardholders can order on 041-772 2281 (24 hr).

In Australia, contact Customer Services, HarperCollins Distribution, Yarrawa Rd, Moss Vale 2577 (tel. [048] 68 0300). **In New Zealand,** contact Customer Services, HarperCollins Publishers, 31 View Rd, Glenfield, Auckland 10 (tel. [09] 444 3740). **In Canada,** contact your local bookshop.

All prices quoted are correct at time of going to press.